Gennaro's
Italian Family
Favourites

Gennaro's
Italian Family
Favourites

Authentic recipes from an Italian kitchen

PAVILION

To my lovely family

This edition published in the United Kingdom in 2015 by
Pavilion
43 Great Ormond Street
London
WC1N 3HZ

ISBN: 978-1-910496-43-5

Illustrations by Sara Mulvanny

A CIP catalogue record for this book is available from the British Library.

10 9 8 7 6 5 4 3 2

Repro by Mission Productions Ltd, Hong Kong
Printed and bound by G Canale & C S.p.A. Italy

Cook's note: all eggs and vegetables are medium unless otherwise stated.

This book can be ordered direct from the publisher at www.pavilionbooks.com

Contents

The family that cooks together stays together

Food brings people together. When I was growing up it was the favourite topic of conversation at the dinner table. This was the same table on which my mother would roll out fresh pasta, knead bread dough or bottle preserves. This table was our altar, a place where all members of our family sat to eat, discuss, argue, laugh, sometimes cry – we had the best of times around it. All my family cooked, including my father, who still liked to make his own meals when he was well into his 90s. My aunts, cousins, neighbours, friends, in fact everyone I knew, cooked – the meals weren't elaborate affairs, but this was good, honest family cooking.

When I first came to England in 1969 I found it odd that food was not a priority in people's lives – they mostly liked to grab a quick bite on the go or eat from a plate balanced on their laps. And, horror of horrors, pasta was out of a can! Of course, things have changed dramatically since then – the immigrants to this country have brought their national dishes and foods and we have been exposed to numerous cooking programmes on television, cookery books and magazines, enticing us to cook and experiment. More recently, with fears of GM foods and intensive farming, we have turned to organic, natural and seasonal produce. When I was young, we ate mainly locally grown food. Nowadays we can find all sorts of exotic things to eat, flown in from around the globe, but I still prefer to eat seasonally. I look forward to the first broad beans and peaches in summer, and some of my favourite produce in autumn – pears, walnuts and chestnuts.

As a parent, I strongly believe in implementing good eating habits from an early age, and showing my kids where our food comes from and how to cook it. I was taught to respect food; the chickens and rabbits we kept were treated humanely. We never wasted food and leftovers were always used. Now my girls really enjoy making bread, pizza, pasta or gnocchi with me, and baking cakes with their mum. They are fascinated to see what I bring home when I've been out hunting; they are not afraid to touch the game birds and aren't squeamish about watching me clean them. When I was old enough, my father would take me hunting – we only killed for food, never for fun – and he taught me a lot. My mother introduced me to wild herbs and mushrooms; I would go with her to the hills above our village of Minori and she would teach me to identify the different species. Food was all around us and dominated our lives. 'Cosa mangiamo per pranzo?' ('What shall we eat for lunch?') was a constant refrain.

Family life in Italy is changing. More women work outside the home, so they no longer have time to prepare fresh pasta and the other traditional dishes their mothers and grandmothers used to make. However, Italians still want to eat well, and even if their fresh pasta is shop-bought they will still try to ensure it's of good quality. Italians still talk about food a lot and, although their meals might be a little more rushed these days, the family still gets together for the evening meal around a table – and certainly always on Sundays.

It is so easy to buy everything ready-made these days that I think we forget we can actually make it ourselves. Take something as basic as bread; not only do my children and I have fun making the dough, watching it rise and enjoying that magical moment when it is baked, but I also know they are eating something good. For me, this is spending quality time with my family – and I am passing on some of my family traditions, which I hope will stay with them forever.

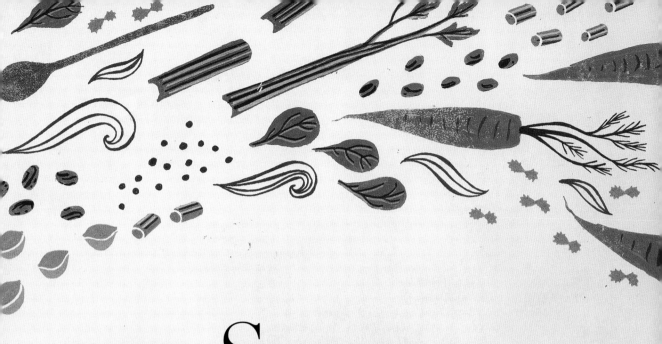

Soup

We loved soup as children, especially during the colder months. My older sisters were the experts. They made soup with beans, pulses, vegetables and all sorts of leftovers – even stale bread. It was perfect comfort food, warming and gentle yet satisfying and full of goodness. We always kept different types of legumi (pulses) in small sacks – borlotti, cannellini, black-eyed, kidney and broad beans, peas and lentils. My sisters would patiently sift through them to discard any impurities and then soak them in cold water overnight before cooking them the next day with vegetables and herbs to make the most delicious, hearty soup. I dedicate this chapter to my elder sisters, Filomena, Genoveffa and Carmelina, for being the best soup-makers ever.

In rural Italy it was common for soup to be made early in the morning and left gently bubbling on the stove until everyone came home in the evening. This ensured an instant warm, home-cooked meal.

Soup is sometimes served instead of pasta or risotto as a primo (starter). For the evening meal, a light soup in the form of a vegetable or meat broth (usually chicken or beef) with small pastina shapes, and a good sprinkling of grated Parmesan is quite common. For a more substantial soup, small ravioli or bread dumplings are added. Pastina in brodo (small pasta shapes in broth) is an Italian favourite, and reminds me of home-cooking in my childhood.

Soups are easy to make, nutritious and economical, and they can be made in large quantities to be frozen and then enjoyed when you have little time to cook, making them nutritious 'fast food'. This is a perfect way to use up seasonal vegetables when you get a glut of, say, courgettes (zucchini), spinach or pumpkin.

I still enjoy soup at home today, and my wife Liz loves to make it – from light pastina broths for the girls and delicate vegetable puréed soups to substantial bean and pasta soups that are a meal in themselves.

Minestra di verdure

Vegetable soup

SERVES 4–6

5 tbsp extra virgin olive oil

1 onion, finely chopped

1 garlic clove, finely chopped

40g/1^1/$_2$ oz pancetta or bacon, finely chopped (optional)

2 potatoes, peeled and cubed

2 carrots, thickly sliced

1 celery stalk, thickly sliced

1 courgette (zucchini), cubed

1 leek, finely chopped

4 cherry tomatoes

100g/3^1/$_2$ oz podded fresh or frozen peas

100g/3^1/$_2$ oz podded fresh or frozen broad (fava) beans

1.5 litres/2^1/$_2$ pints/1^1/$_2$ quarts vegetable stock

250g/9oz ditalini or other small pasta shape

salt and freshly ground black pepper

a few fresh basil leaves, finely chopped

Parmesan, grated, to serve (optional)

- - - - - - - - - - - - - - - - - - -

There is nothing nicer at the end of a long day than a bowl of home-made vegetable soup. I usually throw in whatever fresh vegetables I have, plus frozen peas and broad (fava) beans, which I always keep (of course, in season, it is better to use these fresh, but if you do, add them with the rest of the vegetables at the beginning of the cooking, as they will require longer to cook.) The inclusion of small pasta shapes is to give the soup more bulk, but if you prefer a lighter soup, you can omit them.

Heat the extra virgin olive oil in a large saucepan, add the onion, garlic and pancetta, if using, and sweat, stirring, for 3 minutes. Add all the vegetables, (except the peas and broad beans if using frozen) and mix well. Add the stock and bring to the boil, then half-cover the pan with a lid, lower the heat and simmer gently for 30 minutes (adding the frozen peas and broad beans 10 minutes before the end of the cooking time).

Add the ditalini and cook until the pasta is al dente, following the cooking instructions on the packet. Remove from the heat, season to taste and stir in the basil leaves.

Serve immediately in individual bowls, with freshly grated Parmesan over the top, if desired.

Zuppa di borlotti e osso di prosciutto

Borlotti bean and prosciutto soup

- -

SERVES 4

350g/12oz thick chunks of prosciutto, rinsed

2 large carrots, cut into chunks

2 onions, cut into chunks

2 celery stalks, cut into chunks

3 tomatoes, cut into chunks

2 bay leaves

a handful of fresh parsley, roughly chopped

20 black peppercorns

400g/14oz borlotti beans, cooked, drained and rinsed

55g/2oz Parmesan, grated

extra virgin olive oil, to drizzle

4 slices of country bread, grilled, to serve

- -

In Italy no part of the pig is wasted and it is common to use even the prosciutto bone for soups and stews. The taste is really something else. If I can't get hold of a prosciutto bone, I use thick chunks of prosciutto (which you can ask for at delis) or a piece of gammon (ham). It is a delicious winter warmer and the slightly smoky smell of the prosciutto while cooking takes me back to family evening meals when I was a child. Nowadays, everything fatty seems to be prohibited, but when you make this dish, do include a little of the prosciutto fat – it will really enhance the flavour. If you are using dried borlotti beans, remember to soak them overnight and follow the cooking instructions on the packet. Alternatively, if you are in a hurry, the canned variety will suffice.

Put the prosciutto chunks, all the vegetables, the bay leaves, parsley, peppercorns and 2 litres/3$\frac{1}{2}$ pints/2 quarts water into a large pot. Place on a high heat and bring to the boil, then reduce the heat to medium, half-cover with a lid and cook for 1$\frac{1}{2}$ hours.

Add the borlotti beans and continue to cook for 10 minutes. Preheat the grill (broiler) to medium.

Remove the soup from the heat and divide it between 4 heatproof bowls, then sprinkle 1 tbsp of grated Parmesan on top of each. Place under the grill for a minute, until the cheese has melted slightly. Drizzle with extra virgin olive oil and serve immediately with country bread.

Zuppa di orzo e spinaci

Pearl barley and spinach soup

SERVES 4

200g/7oz pearl barley

4 tbsp extra virgin olive oil, plus extra to drizzle

60g/2¼oz bacon, roughly chopped

2 large potatoes, peeled and cut into chunks

1 garlic clove, peeled and left whole

4 cherry tomatoes, quartered

2 litres/3½ pints/2 quarts hot vegetable stock
(from powder or home-made)

200g/7oz spinach

freshly ground black pepper

Parmesan shavings, to serve

Pearl barley is typically used in soups in northern Italy. When I was growing up we used to have a drink known as orzata, which was made with this grain, but it was on a trip to Scotland during my early years in the UK that I came across it in soup. I have since added it to soups as an alternative to pasta or rice. With the addition of spinach, this is a nutritious and filling meal, which is especially welcome during the colder months.

Rinse the pearl barley in cold water and set aside.

Heat the extra virgin olive oil in a large saucepan, add the bacon, potatoes, garlic and tomatoes and sauté on a medium heat for 1 minute. Add the hot stock and bring to the boil, then reduce the heat to medium-low and simmer for 10 minutes.

Add the pearl barley, half-cover the pan with a lid and cook on a low heat for 1½ hours, until tender (check the instructions on the packet as they may vary). About 5 minutes before the end of the cooking time, add the spinach. Remove from the heat, season with black pepper and serve sprinkled with Parmesan shavings and a drizzle of olive oil.

SERVES 4

1kg/2lb 4oz beef brisket

2 large onions, cut into chunks

2 celery stalks with leaves, cut into big chunks

2 large carrots, cut into big chunks

6 bay leaves

20 black peppercorns

a pinch of salt

200g/7oz pastina

Parmesan, grated, to serve

- - - - - - - - - - - - - - - - -

Pastina in brodo di carne

Beef broth with pastina

Pastina in brodo is comfort food and made by mothers all over Italy. It is light, warming and nourishing, suitable for young children, the elderly and convalescents. I suggest making extra broth to freeze in batches. There are many varieties of *pastina* – conchigliette (small shells), stelline (little stars), farfalline (small butterflies), pepe (peppercorns), alfabeto (alphabet) and tubettini (small tubes). My children have grown up on *pastina in brodo* and they love it; even the older ones still ask for it.

Place the beef, onions, celery, carrots, bay leaf, peppercorns and salt in a large pot with 2.5 litres/4^1/2 pints/2^1/2 quarts water and bring to the boil. Lower the heat, cover with a lid and simmer gently for 2–3 hours, until the meat is tender and falls apart. Skim off the fat, if necessary, during cooking.

Remove the meat and vegetables and set aside. Strain the liquid and pour back into the pan, then bring to the boil, add the *pastina* and cook as directed on the packet.

Remove from the heat and serve in individual bowls with grated Parmesan on top. You can serve the meat and vegetables as a main course if you wish.

Zuppa di pesce di zia Maria

Aunt Maria's fish soup

- -

SERVES 4

500g/1lb 2oz clams, left in salty cold water for 1 hour, then any open clams or broken shells discarded

500g/1lb 2oz mussels, scrubbed and wispy beards pulled off and any open mussels or broken shells discarded

5 tbsp extra virgin olive oil, plus extra to drizzle

2 garlic cloves, finely chopped

$1/2$ red chilli (chile), finely chopped

250g/9oz baby octopuses (thawed if frozen), cleaned and left whole

250g/9oz squid (calamari) (thawed if frozen), cleaned and sliced, head left whole

200ml/7fl oz/scant 1 cup dry white wine

400g can cherry tomatoes

salt

8 king prawns (jumbo shrimp), shell on if you like

2 handfuls of fresh parsley, roughly chopped

200g/7oz fillets of dogfish (also called huss)

4 slices of country bread, grilled and rubbed with garlic, to serve

- -

I would like to recreate my Zia Maria's family fish soup, but my version of it has fewer ingredients than she used. Our family loves fish soup and Zia Maria makes the best. When I was a boy we knew the fishermen well and would end up with all the fish they were unable to sell. I remember this soup bubbling away in the large pot, the aroma wafting through the village. This was always a feast and I would rush home to watch my aunt cook and sometimes help with shelling the mussels and clams. Suddenly all the family would reunite in the kitchen, including our pet dog and cat, all anticipating lunch.

Place the clams in a saucepan, cover with a lid and cook on a high heat for about 3 minutes, or until the shells have opened. Do the same with the mussels. Discard any clams or mussels whose shells remain closed. Scoop out and reserve the flesh of about half the clams and mussels and discard the shells. Keep the remainder in their shells and set aside. Reserve the cooking liquid from both the clams and mussels.

Heat the extra virgin olive oil in a large saucepan, add the garlic and chilli and sweat for 1 minute. Add the octopuses and squid and stir-fry for a minute or so, then add the wine and allow to evaporate. Add the tomatoes and salt to taste, then reduce the heat to medium, cover with a lid and cook for 20 minutes.

Add the prawns and half the parsley and continue to cook for 10 minutes. Add the reserved liquid from the mussels and clams and continue to cook for 5 minutes. Using a wooden spoon, make some room at the bottom of the pan and put in the dogfish fillets. Leave to cook for a couple of minutes, then add the cooked clam and mussel flesh and shellfish and continue to cook for a further 3 minutes, until all of the flavours have infused and the fish is cooked.

Remove from the heat, sprinkle with the remaining parsley and serve with slices of toasted country bread and a drizzle of extra virgin olive oil.

SERVES 4

4 tbsp extra virgin olive oil, plus extra
to drizzle

1 small onion, roughly chopped

600g/1lb 5oz courgettes (zucchini),
thickly sliced

200g/7oz potatoes, peeled and cut
into chunks

750ml/1 pint 6fl oz/3 cups vegetable stock

freshly ground black pepper

a handful of fresh basil leaves

30g/1oz Parmesan, grated

- - - - - - - - - - - - - - - - - - - -

Zuppa di zucchine e basilico
Courgette and basil soup

This soup is simple to prepare and light and delicate in taste, with the freshness of courgettes (zucchini) and basil. Liz cooks it when my friend Paolo has a glut of courgettes in his allotment and she usually makes lots to freeze in batches. It is delicious for all the family, and was ideal when my girls were babies. Serve as a starter or with good bread as a light meal.

Heat the extra virgin olive oil in a medium saucepan, add the onion and courgettes and cook on a medium heat for about 5 minutes. Add the potatoes, stock and some black pepper, increase the heat and bring to the boil. Reduce the heat and simmer gently for 20 minutes.

Remove from the heat and stir in the basil, then blend until smooth. Stir in the Parmesan, heat through if necessary and serve drizzled with extra olive oil.

PASTA

Pasta

For most Italians a day would not be complete without a helping of pasta. When I was a child, my mother and Zia (Aunt) Maria would make fresh pasta at least once a week. It was usually eggless pasta, which is common in southern Italy, rather than the egg variety that is made in the north. They knew instinctively how much flour and water to use. This was always a happy time, as we children would gather round the long kitchen table to watch them roll out the dough and make different shapes. They chatted whilst working, and would tell us off for putting our fingers in the dough. They made the pasta by hand (machines were never used) and it was carefully but swiftly and expertly rolled with a rolling pin. They would use long, thin canes and umbrella spokes to make fusilli and ricci shapes and they made gnocchetti and orecchiette too.

We also had dried pasta, as it provided a quick and nutritious meal. But the ritual weekly pasta-making sessions are times I remember fondly and that pasta always tasted more special.

I still enjoy making pasta. I use a machine to roll out the dough and make shapes such as spaghetti and tagliatelle, while the children make nests with ribbons of pasta. I love to watch their faces as they do this – in between the odd argument as to whose turn it is to turn the handle or make the nests! I also make filled pasta, such as ravioli, tortellini, cappellacci, culurzones, panzerotti and mezzelune, by hand and, of course, the girls love to help.

My home village of Minori in southern Italy has a long tradition of pasta-making. Many small factories opened after the Second World War, employing locals to produce excellent dried pasta. I remember pasta hanging on long canes outside, left to dry in the sun, and the short shapes spread out on white sheets on the ground near the sea. The pasta was then packaged in blue recycled paper and sold. As the industry grew, these small factories closed down and were replaced by larger, famous-named factories in town and cities. But there is still a small family-owned shop in Minori run by my friend

Antonio, who, together with his family, continues to make his own pasta and sell it to the locals.

Ladies from the older generation in Minori, like my great-aunt Antonietta, still get together, just like my mother and zia Maria did all those years ago, and make pasta. Entire afternoons are spent rolling, shaping, chatting, gossiping and producing great, genuine food. When I return home, I love to visit Zia Antonietta (now aged 90) and her friends and watch and admire. I fear this ritual will die away once these ladies are no longer with us, and that's why I like to show my daughters, in the hope they will keep the tradition alive.

Pasta is comfort food to me – it reminds me of home and I know I am eating a nutritious meal. When I felt a little down as a child, my mother would prepare a quick and simple pasta dish to perk me up and it really did the trick. Over the years, scientists have proved that pasta is highly beneficial in our diet – it's an excellent source of carbohydrates, releasing energy slowly, and contains serotonin, a feel-good substance. Although my mother was not a scientist, she knew what was good for me.

You can make pasta as rich or as light as you like, and to suit your budget. In Italy, the traditional family tends to serve it at lunchtime as a primo (starter), followed by a main course of meat or fish. However, it is perfectly acceptable to serve pasta as a main course with, say, a Bolognese ragù or vegetables, fish or pulses for a nutritious meal.

There are numerous pasta shapes – in the region of 600 – to choose from. When I am in Italy I love visiting the supermarkets to marvel at the varieties, all destined for different sauces and dishes. Italians insist that certain pasta shapes go with certain sauces, and they adhere to quite strict rules and regulations. For example, long pasta, such as spaghetti or bucatini, tends to marry well with quick-cook light sauces such as simple tomato or fish. Short shapes, such as penne and fusilli, go with heavier, more robust sauces such as a meat ragù. This is why Italian households usually dedicate a whole kitchen cupboard just to storing dried pasta. When I visit my sister Carmellina in Italy, the pasta packets tumble out of the cupboard as soon as someone opens it. She keeps a selection of long pasta such as spaghetti (which, incidentally, has varying sizes), tagliatelle, linguine and bucatini; short pasta such as penne, farfalle, fusilli and orecchiette; and tiny shapes for soup such as alphabet or stars, especially for her grandchildren – not forgetting lasagne sheets, cannelloni and paccheri for baked dishes made for special occasions. I like to keep a selection in my cupboard too, and I find a couple of varieties in each category is more than enough for our everyday family consumption.

Pasta fresca

Fresh pasta

- - - - - - - - - - - - - - - - - - - -

MAKES 300G/10½OZ

200g/7oz/1⅓ cups '00' flour, plus extra to dust
2 eggs

- - - - - - - - - - - - - - - - - - - -

Fresh pasta can be made by hand simply with a rolling pin, like my mother, grandmothers and aunts did. However, I find it much easier and less time-consuming to use a pasta machine. They are available from kitchen shops and online. For home use, I suggest the small hand machine, but if you regularly make lots of pasta, then it is worth investing in the next size up. You can get electric machines, which mix the dough for you, but these tend to be costly and are very heavy.

Place the flour on a clean work surface or in a large bowl. Make a well in the middle and break in the eggs. Using a fork or your hands, gradually mix the flour with the eggs until combined. Knead for about 5 minutes to form a smooth, soft dough. Shape into a ball, wrap in clingfilm and leave for about 30 minutes, or until you are ready to cook.

Divide the pasta dough into 4 portions and roll each one through your pasta machine, starting at the highest setting. Continue to roll the pasta through the machine; as it gets thinner, turn down the settings until you get to number 1 and your pasta dough is almost wafer-thin.

Place the sheet of pasta on a lightly floured surface and use according to your recipe.

Non-egg fresh pasta

You can make pasta without eggs. Simply substitute 125ml/4fl oz/½ cup hot (not boiling) water for the eggs and follow the method as above.

1 tbsp extra virgin olive oil

30g/1oz/2 tbsp butter

1 small onion, finely chopped

40g/1½oz pancetta or bacon, finely chopped

250g/9oz podded fresh or frozen peas

6 fresh mint leaves (optional)

160ml/5½fl oz/generous ⅔ cup hot vegetable stock

generous 1 tbsp freshly grated Parmesan, plus extra to serve (optional)

salt

300g/10½oz farfalle

Farfalle con pancetta e piselli

Farfalle pasta with pancetta and peas

This quick and easy recipe is especially favoured by my girls. I usually make it with frozen peas, but when in season, fresh peas are ideal – just cook them for a little longer and add a little extra liquid. Farfalle is a butterfly-shaped pasta that will particularly appeal to children.

Gently heat the extra virgin olive oil and butter together in a frying pan until the butter has melted. Increase the heat to medium, add the onion and pancetta and sweat until the onion has softened and the pancetta is golden. Stir in the peas and mint, if using, then add the hot stock and Parmesan, cover with a lid and cook on a medium heat for 3–4 minutes, until the peas are cooked and the water has been absorbed.

Meanwhile, bring a large saucepan of lightly salted water to the boil and cook the farfalle until al dente, according to the instructions on the packet. Drain, add to the sauce and mix well. Serve immediately with an extra sprinkling of Parmesan, if desired.

Orecchiette con zucca e broccoli

Orecchiette pasta with butternut squash and purple sprouting broccoli

- - - - - - - - - - - - - - - - - - -

SERVES 4

3 tbsp extra virgin olive oil, plus extra to drizzle

$1/2$ red onion, finely chopped

$1/2$ garlic clove, finely chopped

85g/3oz pancetta or bacon, finely chopped

1 sprig of fresh thyme

$1/2$ red chilli (chile), finely chopped

250g/9oz butternut squash flesh, cut into cubes

salt

300g/10$1/2$oz orecchiette

100g/3$1/2$oz purple sprouting broccoli, stems trimmed, cut into chunks

30g/1oz Parmesan, grated, plus extra to sprinkle

a pinch of dried chilli (chile) (optional)

- - - - - - - - - - - - - - - - -

Orecchiette, meaning 'little ears', are handmade eggless pasta shapes originating from Puglia and traditionally served with a sauce of broccoli and anchovies. It used to be quite usual to see women in this part of southern Italy sitting outside their homes making this pasta; it is still homemade in many households and my zia Antonietta is a 'professional'. As its popularity has grown, factories have begun producing orecchiette and it is now widely available, even here. I really like this type of pasta; it has quite a bite. This recipe uses butternut squash instead of anchovies, making it an excellent dish for all the family to enjoy. If you like a little heat, add some dried chilli (chile) at the end – it really enhances the squash. I love chilli, but usually just sprinkle it on for my wife Liz and me, and the children have it without.

Heat the extra virgin olive oil in a large frying pan, add the onion, garlic, pancetta, thyme and the fresh chilli and sauté for a couple of minutes. Add the squash, and salt to taste, then lower the heat, cover the pan and cook for about 20 minutes, until tender. Add a couple of tablespoons of hot water if the pumpkin gets too dry.

Meanwhile, bring a large saucepan of lightly salted water to the boil and cook the orecchiette until al dente, according to the instructions on the packet. Drain and set aside.

Cook the broccoli in boiling water for about 5 minutes, until tender, then drain and stir into the cooked pumpkin. Add the drained orecchiette and grated Parmesan and mix well. Serve immediately with a drizzle of extra virgin olive oil, extra Parmesan and the dried chilli, if desired.

4 tbsp extra virgin olive oil

1 garlic clove, squashed but left whole

250g/9oz canned good tuna steak,
drained

a handful of fresh parsley,
finely chopped

2 x 400g cans chopped plum tomatoes

salt and freshly ground black pepper

325g/11½oz tripoline

Tripoline con tonno

Tripoline pasta with tuna

Tripoline is a long, ribbon pasta. It has a curly edge so that it can trap more sauce. It was one of my father's favourite types of pasta, and I remember him serving it with the season's first San Marzano tomatoes, which grew near where we lived, and raw garlic. The taste was unforgettable. I haven't recreated his recipe, as it is difficult to find these tomatoes in England. But roughly at the same time as the San Marzano tomato harvest, the tuna were in season. The boats would come into our small beach and this huge fish was on show for all to see. My mother would always buy a fair amount to preserve in oil, so I decided to combine the tripoline with this very simple store cupboard sauce of canned tuna and tomatoes. Quick and simple to prepare, it makes a nutritious meal for all the family.

Heat the extra virgin olive oil in a large frying pan over a high heat, add the garlic and sauté for 1 minute. Lower the heat to medium, discard the garlic and add the tuna and parsley. Cook for a couple of minutes. Add the tomatoes, salt and pepper and stir well, then cover with a lid and cook on a gentle heat for 20 minutes.

Meanwhile, bring a large saucepan of lightly salted water to the boil and cook the tripoline according to the instructions on the packet. Drain, then add to the sauce, mix well and serve.

SERVES 4

4 tbsp extra virgin olive oil

400g/14oz courgettes (zucchini), sliced

salt and freshly ground black pepper

325g/11½oz spaghetti

4 egg yolks

100ml/3½fl oz/⅓ cup milk

40g/1½oz Parmesan, grated, plus extra
to serve (optional)

a handful of fresh basil leaves, plus a
few to garnish

Spaghetti con zucchine alla carbonara

Spaghetti with courgette carbonara

This is based on the traditional carbonara recipe from Lazio, but I have replaced the *guanciale* (cured pork) with courgettes (zucchini) for a lighter version. I like making this dish as a quick, simple and nutritious midweek meal for the family. The addition of egg yolks is a great way of adding protein if the children are fussy eaters (but do not give raw or undercooked eggs to the very young).

Heat the extra virgin olive oil in a large frying pan, add the courgettes and stir-fry on a high heat until golden and cooked. Remove and drain, discarding the excess oil, then return to the frying pan and set aside.

Meanwhile, bring a large saucepan of lightly salted water to the boil and cook the spaghetti according to the instructions on the packet.

Whisk the egg yolks, milk, Parmesan and salt and pepper to taste in a bowl. Pour into the frying pan with the courgettes, and the basil leaves and heat through gently, stirring, until you have a creamy consistency. Remove from the heat.

Strain the spaghetti, reserving a little of the cooking water. Add the pasta to the sauce and mix well, pouring in a little of the cooking water, if necessary, to loosen the sauce. Garnish with a few basil leaves, sprinkle with grated Parmesan, if desired, and then serve immediately.

Culurzones

Sardinian ravioli filled with cheese, potato and fresh mint

MAKES 30

150g/5¹/₂oz potatoes, peeled and cut into chunks

60g/2¹/₄oz Parmesan, grated

60g/2¹/₄oz pecorino, grated

60g/2¹/₄oz ricotta

2 tbsp finely chopped fresh mint leaves

salt and freshly ground black pepper, to taste

for the pasta

250g/9oz/1²/₃ cups '00' flour, plus extra to dust

1 egg, beaten

for the sauce

100g/3¹/₂ oz/scant ¹/₂ cup butter

8 fresh sage leaves

2 tbsp freshly grated Parmesan

I came across this curious filled pasta many years ago on a visit to Sardinia. The shape intrigues me and can be a bit tricky to master – basically, you seal the dough together by pinching the sides and the result looks similar to a Cornish pasty. There are 9 moves to get it right! When I make fresh pasta at home or at demonstrations, I love to recreate this shape, as it always baffles people. However, if you take it slowly for the first one, it really is quite simple and, once mastered, you will whizz through them and wish you had more pasta to fill. All the family can get involved and see who can be the quickest.

Apart from the intriguing shape, the filling of 3 types of cheese, mashed potato and fresh mint is quite delicious. Believe me, once you start to eat it, you can't stop – but they are filling, so I recommend serving 5 to 6 per person.

For the pasta, put the flour, a pinch of salt, the egg and 100ml/3$\frac{1}{2}$ fl oz/$\frac{1}{3}$ cup water in a bowl and mix well to form a smooth dough. Knead for 10 minutes, wrap in clingfilm and place in the fridge.

For the filling, bring a saucepan of lightly salted water to the boil, add the potatoes and cook for 15–20 minutes, or until tender. Drain well, then mash. Mix in all the remaining filling ingredients.

Remove the clingfilm from the pasta and leave to rest at room temperature for 2 minutes. Cut the dough in half and put each piece through a pasta machine, starting at the highest setting. As the pasta gets thinner, turn down the settings until you have long thin sheets 3mm/$\frac{1}{8}$ inch thick. Place on a lightly floured work surface and, using a 10cm/4-inch pastry cutter, cut out 30 rounds.

To make the culurzones, take a pasta round in one hand, place a full teaspoon of the filling mixture in the centre and gently close in half, then pinch a fold of the dough over from the right and then left side to give a pleated effect (similar to a Cornish pasty). Pinch the top to seal. You will have to work quickly, as the thin pasta tends to dry out.

Bring a large saucepan of lightly salted water to the boil, drop in the culurzones and cook for about 5 minutes, until they rise to the surface and are al dente.

Meanwhile, for the sauce, melt the butter in a large frying pan, then stir in the sage leaves and some of the pasta water. Drain the *culurzones* well, then add them to the butter sauce and mix to coat them well. Sprinkle with Parmesan, remove from the heat and serve immediately.

Cappellacci con zucca

Cappellacci with pumpkin

- - - - - - - - - - - - - - - - - - - -

MAKES ABOUT 40 CAPPELLACCI

1 tbsp extra virgin olive oil

1 sprig of fresh rosemary

175g/6oz pumpkin flesh, cut into cubes

salt and freshly ground black pepper

120g/4¼oz ricotta

4 amaretti biscuits, crushed

1 tsp English mustard

50g/1¾oz Parmesan, grated

for the pasta

400g/14oz/scant 3 cups '00' flour, plus extra
to dust

4 eggs

for the sauce

100g/3½oz/scant ½ cup butter

8 fresh sage leaves

6 tbsp vegetable stock

40g/1½oz Parmesan, grated,
plus extra to serve (optional)

- - - - - - - - - - - - - - - - - - - -

When pumpkins are plentiful I love to make fresh, filled pasta. I normally make *cappellacci*, which translated means 'scruffy hats', because of the shape. The filling originates from northern Italy and is one of those recipes I picked up during my travels throughout the country. The pumpkin adds a lovely sweetness, which is always popular with children and adults alike. Although in Italy this dish would probably be served as a *primo* (starter), I find it is a satisfying main meal.

For the pasta, place the flour on a clean work surface or in a large bowl. Make a well in the middle and break in the eggs. Using a fork or your hands, gradually mix the flour with the eggs until combined. Knead for about 5 minutes to form a smooth, soft dough. Shape into a ball, wrap in clingfilm and leave for about 30 minutes, or until you are ready to cook.

Meanwhile, make the filling. Heat the extra virgin olive oil in a frying pan, add the rosemary and stir-fry on a medium-high heat for 1 minute. Add the pumpkin and salt to taste and stir-fry for 1 minute. Reduce the heat to low, cover with a lid and cook for 12 minutes, until the pumpkin softens. Remove from the heat and mash, then allow to cool. Stir in the ricotta, Amaretti, mustard, Parmesan and salt and pepper. Set aside.

Divide the pasta into 4 portions and use 1 portion at a time, keeping the others wrapped in clingfilm. Preferably using a pasta machine (see page 32), roll out the dough thinly to just under 5mm/¼ inch thick. Place on a lightly floured work surface and cut into 5cm/2 inch squares. Put 1 tsp of the filling in the centre of each square, then fold the pasta over to make a triangle, pressing the sides down firmly to seal (use a little water if it helps). Fold the pointed end over, then bring the 2 opposite corners together around your finger to make a hat shape. Continue like this until you have used all the pasta and filling. Bring a large saucepan of lightly salted water to the boil, then cook the cappellacci for a few minutes, until they rise to the surface.

Meanwhile, for the sauce, melt the butter in a large frying pan, then add the sage leaves, stock and Parmesan. Remove the cooked cappellacci with a slotted spoon and add to the butter sauce, coating the pasta well and taking care not to break it. Serve immediately with more grated Parmesan, if desired.

200g/7oz brown lentils

6 cherry tomatoes

1 large garlic clove, left whole

1 carrot, roughly chopped

a handful of fresh parsley, roughly chopped

1.4 litres/2¼ pints/6 cups cold vegetable stock

2 tbsp extra virgin olive oil, plus extra to serve

400ml/14fl oz/1¾ cups hot water

250g/9oz broken spaghetti

30g/1oz Parmesan, grated, plus extra to serve

Pasta e lenticchie

Lentils with pasta

This is a dish my mother used to make when we were young; then my sister taught Liz how to make it and now we have it at least once a week. Simple to prepare, it is one-pot cooking at its best. Lentils are a good source of protein and iron and, combined with the pasta, make an ideal meal. Use small brown lentils, such as the Castelluccio variety, which keep their shape during cooking and don't become mushy like the larger lentils. I have used broken-up spaghetti, or you could use shapes like tubettini or ditalini. In Italy, we often add some sausage or pieces of cured pork to give the dish extra flavour.

Place the lentils, tomatoes, garlic, carrot, half the parsley and all the stock in a large saucepan. Bring to the boil, then lower the heat, half-cover with a lid and simmer gently for 25–30 minutes, until the lentils are tender. About 5 minutes before the end of cooking time, add the extra virgin olive oil.

Add the hot water and return to the boil, then add the broken spaghetti, lower the heat to medium and simmer until the spaghetti is cooked.

Remove from the heat and stir in the Parmesan. Serve with a drizzle of extra virgin olive oil and extra Parmesan, if desired.

SERVES 4

400g can of cannellini beans, drained
and rinsed

250g/9oz cherry tomatoes, quartered

2 tbsp extra virgin olive oil

salt and freshly ground black pepper

360g/12¹/₂ oz conchiglie

for the pesto

70g/2¹/₂oz wild rocket (arugula)

40g/1¹/₂oz Parmesan, grated

100ml/3¹/₂fl oz/¹/₃ cup extra virgin
olive oil

Conchiglie al pesto di rucola e fagioli cannellini

Conchiglie with rocket pesto and cannellini beans

This is easy to make and perfect for the warmer spring months, when wild rocket (arugula) is plentiful. I like to enlist the help of the girls to collect this versatile leaf. Of course, supermarkets now stock wild rocket all year round, cleaned and ready to use.

To make the pesto, place the rocket, Parmesan and extra virgin olive oil in a blender and whizz to a fairly smooth sauce. Set aside.

In a bowl, mix together the beans, cherry tomatoes, extra virgin olive oil and salt and pepper to taste.

Bring a large saucepan of lightly salted water to the boil and cook the conchiglie until al dente, according to the instructions on the packet. Drain, place in a large bowl and combine with the pesto, beans and tomatoes. Check for seasoning and, if necessary, add more salt and pepper. Serve immediately or serve cold.

Bucatini alle melanzane

Bucatini with aubergine

- - - - - - - - - - - - - - - - - - -

SERVES 4

175ml/6fl oz/³/₄ cup extra virgin olive oil

400g/14oz aubergine (eggplant), cut into
thin strips

2 garlic cloves, finely chopped

¹/₂ red chilli (chile), thinly sliced

a pinch of dried oregano

2 x 400g cans chopped plum tomatoes

a handful of fresh basil leaves, roughly
chopped, plus extra to garnish

8 anchovy fillets in oil, drained

salt and freshly ground black pepper

350g/12oz bucatini

3 tbsp capers

85g/3oz pitted black olives, sliced

- - - - - - - - - - - - - - - - - - -

This southern Italian dish has always been a family favourite and was usually cooked during summer. During this time of year we would be surrounded by aubergines and we would cook them in many dishes, as well as preserve them for our store cupboard. I remember my mother saying the best aubergine is the 'cime di viola', a long, thin, bright purple, seedless variety. When I see them here in the market I always buy them. Last year a friend had a glut of this variety in his allotment and gave me some – they had a really special taste. If you come across them during summer, I urge you to try them.

Heat 6 tbsp extra virgin olive oil in a large frying pan, add the aubergine and stir-fry on a medium heat for about 10 minutes, until golden-brown and cooked through. The oil will be absorbed quickly, but don't add more – when the aubergines are cooked the oil will exude from them. Remove, drain on kitchen towel and set aside.

Heat the remaining oil in the frying pan, add the garlic, chilli and oregano and sweat on a medium heat for 1 minute. Add the tomatoes and basil and cook for 15 minutes. Add the anchovies and cook for 5 minutes, stirring from time to time.

Meanwhile, bring a large saucepan of lightly salted water to the boil and cook the bucatini until al dente, according to the instructions on the packet. Drain and stir into the tomato sauce, then add the cooked aubergines and the capers and olives, toss well and serve immediately with a few fresh basil leaves.

Fusilli con datterini e olive taggiasche

Fusilli with baby vine tomatoes and taggiasca olives

This dish can be eaten warm or made in advance to enjoy cold as a salad – perfect for a family picnic! The kids will love the fusilli shape and, even if they are not keen on olives and onion, they will enjoy picking at the healthy tomatoes. If you can't find baby vine tomatoes, substitute cherry tomatoes. I love the unique taste of Ligurian taggiasca olives, which can be found in good Italian delis; but Kalamata olives make a fine substitute, and are widely available.

Combine the tomatoes, olives, onion, extra virgin olive oil and some salt and pepper in a large bowl, cover and set aside.

Bring a large saucepan of lightly salted water to the boil and cook the fusilli until al dente, according to the instructions on the packet. Drain well and add to the tomato mixture, tossing well. Scatter the basil leaves over and either serve immediately or enjoy cold as a pasta salad. Drizzle with a little extra virgin olive oil just before serving.

4 tbsp extra virgin olive oil

$1/2$ onion, grated

1 small carrot, grated

$1/2$ courgette, grated

6 fresh basil leaves (optional)

500ml/18fl oz/generous 2 cups passata
(strained tomatoes)

2 tsp vegetable stock powder

salt and freshly ground black pepper

300g/10$1/2$oz penne

Parmesan, grated, to serve (optional)

Penne al pomodoro e verdurine

Penne with tomato and vegetables

This is my wife Liz's recipe, and she has made it for our daughters since they were very young. It's perfect for kids, and the vegetables can be blended into a smooth sauce if they prefer. You can make a lot and freeze it in batches, as we often do, for a quick, nutritious meal when you're pressed for time. Of course, it's delicious for grown-ups too!

Heat the extra virgin olive oil in a saucepan, add the grated vegetables and sweat on a medium heat for 3–4 minutes, until the onion has softened. Stir in the basil leaves, if you like, and the passata and powdered stock. Bring to a simmer, then reduce the heat to low, cover with a lid and cook for 25 minutes. Check for seasoning.

Meanwhile, bring a large saucepan of lightly salted water to the boil and cook the penne until al dente, according to the instructions on the packet. Drain, then add to the sauce and mix well. Serve immediately with grated Parmesan, if desired.

For older babies and toddlers

Omit the stock powder. Blend the sauce, once it's cooked, to a smooth purée. If you're doing this, there's no need to grate the vegetables, simply roughly chop, but remember to increase the cooking time for the larger pieces of vegetables.

Pasti Veloci

Quick Meals

It's a shame that some people think a quick meal has to be shop-bought and ready-made, something you pop in the microwave. Of course it's much harder to cook from fresh these days, with most adults working and often facing a long commute home. Even in Italy, the land of the cooking mamma, people don't have time to prepare the two- or three-course meals their mothers used to make. However, ready-meals are expensive, and most contain high levels of fat, salt and sugar. And there is nothing nicer than sitting down to a home-cooked meal, whether it's a lavish affair or simply a bowl of pasta with home-made tomato sauce. It is nutritious, tasty and satisfying for all the family.

Pasta can be rustled up quickly, but there are other easy dishes that can be made in no time and that add variety to your diet. Risotto is the favourite in our house, and I use whatever ingredients we have: peas, courgettes (zucchini), carrots, broad (fava) beans, pumpkin; sometimes, if the fridge is bare, I serve it simply with butter and lots of Parmesan. Thinly sliced steak and scaloppine of veal, served with vegetables or salad, are also popular, and take little time to cook on the grill pan.

Chicken is quick to cook too, and if you get little pieces such as thighs, they can be roasted in a hot oven with small potato chunks, seasoned with garlic and rosemary, in less than half an hour; serve with steamed broccoli or green beans and you have a wonderful, nutritious meal with hardly any effort. Frittata is quick to make too, and a great source of protein. I add whatever is to hand, for instance cheese, prosciutto, pancetta, peas, courgettes and onions. I often make a big frittata and enjoy a slice the next day in a sandwich. Fish is also quick to cook, and one of the nicest ways to prepare it is to steam white fillets and drizzle them with extra virgin olive oil and lemon juice. Served with boiled baby potatoes, or mash for the kids, and green vegetables, this is a lovely healthy and light meal for everyone.

I believe with a well-stocked store cupboard and fridge, you can serve good, well-balanced, nutritious meals every day with a minimum of time and effort.

Risotto

Risotto is a predominately northern Italian dish, but we still enjoy eating rice in the south, and my mother would make her own version of risotto with lots of vegetables. The difference was in the cooking method – she would never stand by the pot stirring, as you should when making a traditional risotto. She would place rice, vegetables, some olive oil and lots of stock in a pot and let it bubble very gently until the rice was cooked and had absorbed all the liquid. She added olive oil and a little pecorino cheese at the end, but never butter and Parmesan. The result was less creamy than a normal risotto, but still very tasty.

I discovered 'real' risotto when I began working as a chef and travelled to northern Italian regions, where rice is cultivated. Here I learned that a number of types of rice work well in risotto (see page 62), as long as you use just one variety.

Like pasta, risotto in Italy tends to be served as a *primo* (starter) and can be combined with a variety of ingredients. It is often made with saffron (a traditional dish of Lombardy), mushrooms, or one of many vegetables, beans and pulses. It can be made simply, with butter and Parmesan or, for a lavish occasion, with shellfish and truffles.

I enjoy making risotto for the family – it's quick and nutritious and the favourite meal of my daughters Chloe and Olivia. I can guarantee clean plates when we've had risotto and it makes me happy to know they have eaten well. But they also enjoy getting involved and love to help with the stirring.

SERVES 4

1.5 litres/2$\frac{1}{2}$ pints/1$\frac{1}{2}$ quarts vegetable
or chicken stock (from powder or
home-made)
3 tbsp extra virgin olive oil
1 onion, finely chopped
375g/13oz/scant 2 cups arborio rice
50g/1$\frac{3}{4}$oz/4 tbsp butter
50g/1$\frac{3}{4}$oz Parmesan, grated
salt and freshly ground black pepper

Risotto

Basic risotto

The first rule of risotto-making is to use the correct Italian rice – arborio, carnaroli or vialone nano. Do not use any other type, as the risotto will not work. Next, use good stock: home-made is ideal, but a good cube or powder will suffice. Your stock can be any type, depending on the ingredients in your risotto; for a basic risotto I use vegetable or chicken. Keep the stock gently simmering on the hob while you are adding it to the rice, as it must be added hot or the risotto will stop cooking. You may find you will need a little more or less than I have used in this recipe, as it will be affected by how you cook. Keep stirring the risotto or it may stick to the pan, and cook it gently on a low heat, making sure that all the liquid has been absorbed before you add the next ladleful. Once the risotto is cooked, the pan must be removed from the heat before you add the butter and Parmesan. If you follow these rules and stir for about 20 minutes, there is no reason why you shouldn't have a perfect risotto.

Put the stock in a saucepan and leave it gently simmering on a low heat.

Heat the extra virgin olive oil in a heavy-based saucepan. Add the onion and sweat on a medium heat until softened. Stir in the rice with a wooden spoon and coat each grain with the oil. Add a couple of ladles of hot stock and cook, stirring continuously, until the stock is absorbed. Add more stock and repeat. Continue adding stock, cooking and stirring in this way for about 20 minutes, until the rice is cooked. It should be soft on the outside but al dente on the inside.

Remove from the heat and, with a wooden spoon, beat in the butter and Parmesan until the ingredients are well combined and creamy. In Italy, this is known as *mantecare*. Check for seasoning and, if necessary, add salt and freshly ground black pepper. Serve immediately.

1.5 litres/2¹/₂ pints/1¹/₂ quarts vegetable
stock (from powder or home-made)

3 tbsp extra virgin olive oil

1 small onion, finely chopped

¹/₂ celery stalk, finely chopped

1 small carrot, finely chopped

1 bay leaf

200g/7oz minced (ground) pork

200g/7oz savoy cabbage heart, sliced

375g/13oz/scant 2 cups arborio rice

125ml/4fl oz/¹/₂ cup dry white wine

50g/1³/₄oz/4 tbsp butter

50g/1³/₄oz Parmesan, grated

salt and freshly ground black pepper

- - - - - - - - - - - - - - - - - - - -

Risotto con carne macinata

Risotto with minced pork and savoy cabbage

This is a lovely way of using minced meat; it blends perfectly with risotto. This dish is a favourite quick and simple midweek meal in our house. I find pork mince very flavoursome, but you can use minced beef or a combination of the two.

Put the stock in a saucepan and leave it gently simmering on a low heat.

Heat the extra virgin olive oil in a medium, heavy-based saucepan. Add the onion, celery and carrot and sweat on a medium heat until softened. Add the bay leaf and mince, increase the heat to medium-high, and cook until the mince has browned all over. Add the cabbage, lower the heat back to medium and cook, stirring, for 1 minute. Stir in the rice with a wooden spoon and coat each grain with the oil. Add a couple of ladles of hot stock and cook, stirring continuously, until the stock is absorbed. Add more stock and repeat. Continue adding stock, cooking and stirring in this way for about 20 minutes, until the rice is cooked. It should be soft on the outside but al dente on the inside.

Remove from the heat and, with a wooden spoon, beat in the butter and Parmesan until the ingredients are well combined and creamy. Check for seasoning and, if necessary, add salt and freshly ground black pepper. Serve immediately.

Risotto con asparagi, zucchini e piselli

Risotto with asparagus, courgette and peas

SERVES 4

1.2 litres/2 pints/5 cups vegetable stock (from powder or home-made)

4 tbsp extra virgin olive oil

1 small onion, finely chopped

350g/12oz/1^{3}/$_{4}$ cups arborio rice

125ml/4fl oz/^{1}/$_{2}$ cup dry white wine

1 courgette (zucchini), cut into small cubes

8 asparagus stems, finely chopped (discard any hard stems)

100g/3^{1}/$_{2}$oz podded fresh or frozen peas

30g/1oz/2 tbsp butter

40g/1^{1}/$_{2}$oz Parmesan, grated

I dedicate this risotto to my daughters Chloe and Olivia, who love it. I like to make it in late spring when the vegetables are tender and at their best. Out of season, I use frozen peas and substitute other vegetables – perhaps carrots and frozen broad (fava) beans – for the fresh vegetables. It's a quick and simple one-pot meal that all the family will love.

Pour the stock into a saucepan, bring it to the boil, then reduce the heat to low and leave it gently simmering.

Heat the extra virgin olive oil in a heavy-based saucepan. Add the onion and sweat on a medium heat until softened. Stir in the rice with a wooden spoon and coat each grain with the oil. Add the wine and allow to evaporate, stirring all the time. Stir in the courgette, asparagus and peas. Add a couple of ladles of hot stock and, stirring continuously, cook until the stock is absorbed. Add more stock and repeat. Continue adding stock, cooking and stirring in this way for about 20 minutes, until the rice is cooked. It should be soft on the outside but al dente on the inside.

Remove from the heat and beat in the butter and Parmesan with a wooden spoon. Leave to rest for 1 minute, then serve.

4 tbsp extra virgin olive oil

4 thin sirloin steaks, each about 150g/5^1/$_2$oz

1 garlic clove, thinly sliced

4 anchovy fillets in oil, drained

1 tbsp capers

a handful of fresh parsley, finely chopped

400g can chopped plum tomatoes

1 tsp dried oregano

salt and freshly ground black pepper

Bistecche alla pizzaiola

Steak in tomato sauce

This dish was a very popular quick meal in our household when I was a child. The tomato sauce was often served with pasta as a starter and then we would eat the meat afterwards. If you don't want pasta with it, serve it with lots of good bread to mop up the sauce.

Heat the extra virgin olive oil in a large shallow frying pan and fry the steaks for 1–2 minutes on each side to seal the meat. Remove and set aside.

Add the garlic, anchovies, capers and half the parsley and stir-fry for a couple of minutes. Add the tomatoes and oregano, stirring well, and cook on a high heat for 1 minute. Lower the heat, return the steaks to the pan, making sure they are covered with tomato sauce, and cook for 10–15 minutes, depending on the thickness of the meat. Check for seasoning and, if necessary, add salt and pepper. Remove from the heat, sprinkle on the remaining parsley and serve immediately.

4 veal escalopes (scallops), each
about 150g/5¹/₂oz

a little plain (all-purpose) flour, to dust

85g/3oz/6 tbsp butter

for the sauce

30g/1oz capers, finely chopped

4 anchovy fillets in oil, drained and
finely chopped

50g/1³/₄oz/scant 4 tbsp softened butter

Scaloppine con salsa di capperi

Veal escalope with a caper sauce

This is a version of the traditional *scaloppine al limone* (with lemon), which is very popular in Italy – the caper paste enhancing the veal. This makes a quick and simple main course for all the family. You can, if you prefer, substitute pork escalopes (scallops) for the veal. If using pork you may need to increase the cooking time slightly, depending on the thickness.

Mix all the sauce ingredients together to make a paste, then wrap in clingfilm and set aside in a cool place.

Dust the veal in the flour. Heat the 85g/3oz/3 tbsp butter in a large frying pan. Add the veal and fry on a medium heat for about 4 minutes on each side, until cooked through. Remove and set aside.

Add the caper mixture to the pan and cook, stirring, on a high heat until you have a creamy sauce. Pour over the veal slices and serve immediately.

SERVES 4

1kg/2lb 4oz white fish fillets, such as
cod, hake or plaice

a strip of unwaxed lemon rind

baby potatoes, boiled, to serve

green beans, boiled, to serve

for the dressing

6 tbsp extra virgin olive oil

juice of 1 large lemon

2 garlic cloves, thinly sliced (optional)

a handful of fresh parsley,
finely chopped

salt

Pesce del pontile

White fish with lemon and olive oil dressing

When I was growing up, fish was abundant and we would eat it often. The local fishermen taught me the tricks of the trade, and we ate the best and freshest produce. This is my favourite way of cooking white fish. Quick and easy to prepare, it is a light but nutritious meal for all the family, served with boiled or mashed potatoes and green beans. If you prefer, you can omit the garlic.

Rinse the fish under cold running water, then place in a pan with the lemon rind and enough water to cover the fillets. Bring to the boil, then reduce the heat to medium and simmer for 10–15 minutes, or until the fish is cooked through.

Meanwhile, combine all the ingredients for the dressing and beat with a small hand whisk until well amalgamated.

Carefully drain the fish, place it on a serving dish and pour the dressing over it, then leave it to rest for a couple of minutes. Serve with boiled baby potatoes and green beans.

Sgombri farciti

Filled mackerel

SERVES 4

4 mackerel, scaled, gutted and cleaned
1 tbsp plain (all-purpose) flour, to dust
a pinch of fresh oregano
a pinch of fennel seeds
300ml/10fl oz/1¼ cups vegetable oil
lemon wedges, to serve

for the filling

85g/3oz black olives, pitted and finely chopped
2 garlic cloves, finely chopped
30g/1oz capers, finely chopped
4 anchovy fillets in oil, drained and finely chopped
1 tbsp finely chopped fresh parsley
1 tsp finely grated unwaxed lemon zest

Mackerel is a nutritious fish, and good value too. The mixture for the filling really gives a kick to the fish. Simple to make and quick to cook, this is an ideal, healthy midweek supper for all the family.

Combine all the filling ingredients in a bowl and use to stuff the cavity of each fish. Secure with raffia or kitchen string, making sure the filling cannot escape.

Combine the flour, oregano and fennel seeds on a plate and dust the mackerel with the mixture. Heat the oil in a large frying pan until a piece of bread dropped in sizzles immediately, add the filled mackerel and cook on a high heat for about 4 minutes on each side. Lower the heat, cover with a lid and continue to cook for 3 minutes, until the fish is cooked through. Remove and serve with lemon wedges.

SERVES 4

1kg/2lb 4oz chicken thighs and drumsticks
salt and freshly ground black pepper
a little plain (all-purpose) flour, to dust
150ml/5fl oz/²/₃ cup extra virgin olive oil
a bulb of garlic, cloves divided and skins left on
a large handful of fresh rosemary, broken in half
150ml/5fl oz/²/₃ cup dry white wine

for the bruschetta
a few slices of bread
a few garlic cloves, peeled

Pollo con aglio e rosmarino servito con bruschetta

Chicken with garlic, rosemary and bruschetta

This is a good old rustic chicken dish, full of flavour, which I love to make when I have friends round for a simple meal. It's easy to prepare, with just a few basic ingredients, and is made in just one large pan. This is exactly how we used to cook it at home at olive oil harvest time. Use good extra virgin olive oil, as you need quite a lot and the flavour of the dish is really enhanced by it. It's excellent served with the bruschetta.

Season the chicken with salt and pepper and dust with plain flour. Put the extra virgin olive oil in a large heavy-based frying pan and place on a medium-high heat. When hot, add the floured chicken and seal well for 1–2 minutes on each side, until golden brown and quite crisp. Reduce the heat to medium-low, add the garlic and rosemary, cover with a lid and cook for 30 minutes, turning the chicken from time to time. Raise the heat to high, remove the lid, add the wine and simmer until it has evaporated. Check the chicken is cooked; the flesh should come away easily from the bone and there should be no sign of pink when you pierce the thickest part. Skim the oil from the top and set aside.

For the bruschetta, grill the bread, then immediately rub them with the garlic and drizzle with a little of the reserved oil. Serve the chicken with the bruschetta.

salt

200g/7oz quick-cook polenta
(cornmeal)

50g/1³/₄oz/scant 4 tbsp butter

75g/2³/₄oz Parmesan, grated

100g/3¹/₂oz fontina, cut into small cubes

200g/7oz gorgonzola, sliced into four

Polenta concia con gorgonzola

Polenta with gorgonzola

Polenta (cornmeal) is maize flour, and has always been a staple in northern Italy, especially in rural areas. It has become popular all over the country as well as abroad, and is now served in top restaurants.

Traditionally, polenta took about 40 minutes to cook and required constant stirring. Nowadays, you can buy *polenta svelta* (quick polenta), which takes no longer than 5 minutes to cook. When I was a boy, my mother would stir in lots of cheese for extra flavour and nourishment. This recipe is from my wife Liz's family, who come from northern Italy, and it is served with a slice of gorgonzola on top. It's a quick winter warmer for all the family.

Pour 1 litre/1³/₄ pints/4 cups water into a medium saucepan, add a pinch of salt and bring to the boil. Gradually add the polenta, stirring all the time, until it is amalgamated. Reduce the heat (polenta does tend to bubble quite a bit), and beware of any lumps forming. If they do, just beat very energetically until they are dissolved. Stir the polenta for about 5 minutes, or according to the instructions on the packet. Add the butter, Parmesan and fontina and mix well, until amalgamated. Divide the polenta between 4 plates and top each with a slice of the gorgonzola. Serve immediately.

extra virgin olive oil, to grease

250g/9oz ricotta

1 egg yolk

3 tbsp freshly grated Parmesan

1 tbsp finely chopped fresh parsley

1 tsp finely grated unwaxed lemon zest

60g/2¼oz/scant ½ cup dried breadcumbs

1 quantity of basic tomato sauce, to serve (see page 79)

Polpette di ricotta e limone al forno

Baked ricotta and lemon dumplings

These meat-free meatballs are delicious. My mother often made them when we had lots of ricotta, or when meat was forbidden for religious purposes, such as during Lent. She would enhance the flavour with the addition of Amalfi lemon zest. They can be served with a tomato sauce if desired. Quick and easy to make, they are sure to appeal to children.

Preheat the oven to 180°C/350°F/gas mark 4. Lightly grease a baking sheet.

Combine all the remaining ingredients, apart from the tomato sauce, in a bowl. Shape into small balls roughly the size of walnuts and place on the baking sheet. Bake for 15–20 minutes, until slightly golden.

Reheat the tomato sauce in a saucepan and serve with the meatballs.

Frittata di cipolle e zucchini

Onion and courgette omelette

- -

SERVES 4

4 tbsp extra virgin olive oil, plus a little extra if
necessary

2 onions, thinly sliced

1 courgette (zucchini), thinly sliced

6 eggs

40g/1½oz Parmesan, grated

salt and freshly ground black pepper

- -

A simple, nutritious meal, often made as a main course in Italy. We would have an omelette like this for a quick meal or during religious periods when meat was forbidden, such as on Friday or during Lent. It can be served hot or cold – even taken on picnics – or just eaten with bread as a sandwich. In season, you could use the large spring onions (scallions), which give freshness to the omelette.

Heat the extra virgin olive oil in a frying pan. Add the onions and courgette and sweat on a medium heat until softened.

Meanwhile, beat the eggs, Parmesan and salt and pepper to taste in a bowl. If necessary, add a little more oil to the pan, then pour in the egg mixture. Cook on a medium heat for about 5 minutes, until the bottom of the omelette is golden. Turn the omelette over and cook the other side for about 3 minutes, until golden. Remove from the heat, cut into quarters and serve.

SERVES 4

2 tbsp extra virgin olive oil
1 garlic clove, finely chopped
400g can chopped plum tomatoes
8 fresh basil leaves, roughly torn
salt and freshly ground black pepper

Salsa al pomodoro

Basic tomato sauce

Quick and simple to prepare, this light tomato sauce is indispensable for dressing pasta and gnocchi, and it makes an ideal accompaniment to *Polpette di ricotta* (see page 77). I suggest making lots of it and freezing it in batches – that way you will always have the basis for a quick meal.

Heat the extra virgin olive oil in a saucepan, add the garlic and sweat for a couple of minutes, taking care not to burn it. Add the tomatoes, basil and some salt and pepper and simmer gently for 20 minutes. Remove from the heat and use according to your recipe.

pasti à Lunga Cottura

Slow
Meals

Whealen there is time, perhaps at the weekends or during holidays, I love to cook traditionally. It's good to slow down, know that I am not cooking in a restaurant kitchen or on a photo shoot, and recreate some of the dishes of my childhood. On cold days I cook huge pots of stew. Once the preparation has been done, I get on with other things or relax while the meat and vegetables gently bubble away on the stove and the cooking smells drift through the house. This is usually when one of the girls will notice and try to guess what's for dinner.

I love to eat anything made with beans or pulses – borlotti beans, cannellini beans, broad (fava) beans, peas, chickpeas, or green, red and brown lentils, as well as many others. They remind me of my childhood home in Italy, where they were a regular feature at dinner during the winter. Like my family, I use dried beans and pulses (but I do keep the odd can in my store cupboard for quick meals); I love soaking them in cold water the night before a meal in anticipation of what I might cook the next day, wondering what herbs and other ingredients we have available to flavour them with. Not only are beans and pulses very nutritious, fat-free and a good source of protein, they are also economical and delicious.

The girls love to help out in the kitchen, and we sometimes make gnocchi, fresh pasta or dough for bread and pizza together. They both adore sausages, so I showed them our simple family recipe for home-made sausages (see page 100) and now they want to make it all the time. Baked pasta and Parmigiana dishes are also favourites, and are good ways of using up leftover salami, cheese, tomato sauce and vegetables. They go a long way too – 1 large aubergine (eggplant) is more than enough to feed 4 people in a delicious and nourishing Parmigiana di melanzane. Filled and baked vegetables – (bell) peppers, courgettes (zucchini), onions or aubergines – are equally good; a mix of cheese, ham or salami and stale bread, or minced meat, will turn these humble vegetables into really filling and nutritious main meals.

Gnocchi

Gnocchi has northern Italian roots, but the south has its own versions. In fact, the speciality of my village of Minori is *ndundari*, a type of gnocchi made with ricotta instead of potatoes. It was traditionally eaten on special feast days, when my mother would lovingly make it for us, coated in a light tomato sauce. I make it at home now and have converted my wife Liz, who would happily eat it every day.

The most common gnocchi is made with potatoes and, judging by how many packets are sold in supermarkets in the UK and throughout Europe, like pasta, it is conquering the world.

I prefer to make my own gnocchi, getting all the family involved in the preparation. The girls love to help – mashing the potatoes, rolling out the dough and cutting it into the small shapes. Gnocchi are simple to make and a great thing to do with the family on a wet weekend. The ingredients of potatoes, flour and eggs are economical and storecupboard basics, and it's not only fun to make, but the result is so much softer and tastier than the shop-bought variety. I think the experience makes you appreciate good food more and brings you closer together as a family. Children like gnocchi, and its soft texture makes it ideal for toddlers.

You can make variations of gnocchi – for instance, adding chestnut flour to give a slightly sweet flavour (which I love because I'm mad about chestnuts). Pumpkin gnocchi is popular in northern Italy, and is made using mashed pumpkin instead of potatoes. *Gnocchi alla Romana* is made with semolina flour and baked. Gnocchi can also be stuffed, perhaps with mushrooms or vegetables, but it will be extremely filling.

Whichever gnocchi you prefer, it is substantial and, although in Italy it is served as a *primo* (starter), I like to have it as a single course combined with a light sauce such as pesto or tomato, or simply with butter and Parmesan.

Gnocchi di patate

Potato gnocchi

SERVES 4–6

1kg/2lb 4oz floury potatoes such as King Edwards, roughly all same size, scrubbed

salt

1 egg

300g/10½oz/generous 2 cups plain (all-purpose) flour

rice flour, to dust

Rice flour is better than plain flour for rolling out gnocchi as it prevents the dough from sticking.

Put the unpeeled potatoes in a saucepan with lots of cold water, bring to the boil and cook for 15–20 minutes, or until they are tender but not falling apart. Drain, allow to cool slightly, then remove the skins. While warm, mash the potatoes and leave to cool.

Place the mash in a large bowl, season with salt, stir in the egg, add the flour and work to a soft dough. Sprinkle the rice flour over a work surface and roll out the dough into long sausage shapes. Using a sharp knife, cut into 2cm/¾ inch lengths. Set aside.

Bring a large saucepan of lightly salted water to the boil. Drop the gnocchi into the water in batches and simmer for a minute or so, until they rise to the top. Remove with a slotted spoon and drain well, then add to a sauce of your choice. Mix well and serve.

SERVES 4–6

1 quantity of potato gnocchi (see page 86)

Parmesan, grated, to serve (optional)

for the Bolognese ragù

2 tbsp extra virgin olive oil

1 small onion, finely chopped

1 small carrot, finely chopped

200g/7oz minced (ground) beef

200g/7oz minced (ground) pork

salt

400g can chopped plum tomatoes

Gnocchi di patate con ragù Bolognese

Potato gnocchi with Bolognese ragù sauce

This is slow comfort food at its best, a perfect winter warmer for when the children are at home to help make the gnocchi. You can, of course, make the Bolognese ragù in advance – as long as the meat has not been previously frozen, it is an ideal sauce to freeze. Filling, nutritious and fun to prepare, this dish will surely be a winner for all the family.

For the Bolognese ragù, heat the extra virgin olive oil in a large saucepan, add the onion and carrot and sweat for a couple of minutes. Add the minced (ground) meats and stir-fry for 3–4 minutes, until browned all over. Season with salt. Add the tomatoes, then fill the empty can with water and pour this into the pan. Lower the heat, cover with a lid and simmer gently for 2 hours, stirring from time to time.

Meanwhile, make and cook the potato gnocchi according to the recipe on page 86.

Add the gnocchi to the Bolognese ragù and mix carefully. Remove from the heat and serve with a sprinkling of grated Parmesan, if desired.

Gnocchi di patate con pesto

Potato gnocchi with pesto sauce

SERVES 4–6

1 quantity of potato gnocchi (see page 86)

for the pesto sauce
2 tbsp pine kernels

1 garlic clove

$^1/_2$ tsp coarse sea salt

85g/3oz fresh basil leaves

200ml/7fl oz/scant 1 cup good extra virgin olive oil

2 tbsp freshly grated Parmesan, plus extra to serve

Pesto marries well with gnocchi and the basil sauce really enhances the potato. Children will love to grind the ingredients for the pesto in a pestle and mortar and see them transformed into a silky smooth sauce. This is a lighter way of serving gnocchi, but equally satisfying. Pesto can be made in advance and kept in the fridge for about a week.

Make and cook the potato gnocchi according to the recipe on page 86.

For the pesto, place the pine kernels, garlic and sea salt in a mortar and grind to a paste with a pestle. Add a few basil leaves and some extra virgin olive oil, grinding and stirring with the pestle all the time. Repeat until you have used up all the basil and about half the oil and the pesto has a fairly smooth silky consistency. Add the remaining oil and the Parmesan and stir to combine. (Alternatively, you can place all the ingredients in a food processor and blend – although this is not as much fun and you lose the slight crunchiness of the pine kernels.)

Place the gnocchi in a large serving dish or on individual plates. Pour over the pesto and mix well, taking care not to break the gnocchi. Serve immediately, with a sprinkling of grated Parmesan, if desired.

SERVES 4–6

1 quantity of potato gnocchi
(see page 86)

for the sauce
100g/3¹/₂oz/scant ¹/₂ cup butter
8 fresh sage leaves
1 tbsp freshly grated Parmesan,
plus extra to serve

Gnocchi con burro e salvia

Gnocchi with a butter and sage sauce

Plain and simple, but totally delicious. The addition of sage gives this a lovely flavour, but if you're cooking it for children, they may prefer just butter and Parmesan, as sage can be a little overpowering.

Make and cook the potato gnocchi according to the recipe on page 86.

Place a large frying pan on a medium heat and melt the butter, then add the sage leaves and stir in the Parmesan. Add the gnocchi, with a little of the cooking water.

Sauté for 1 minute, making sure that all the gnocchi are coated in the butter sauce. Serve immediately, with a sprinkling of grated Parmesan, if desired.

Zucchini ripieni al forno con salsa al pomodoro

Baked filled courgettes in tomato sauce

SERVES 4–6

6 large courgettes (zucchini)

2 tbsp extra virgin olive oil

1 garlic clove, finely chopped

150g/5$\frac{1}{2}$oz minced (ground) beef

150g/5$\frac{1}{2}$oz minced (ground) pork

100g/3$\frac{1}{2}$oz stale white bread, soaked in a little water and squeezed

1 egg

30g/1oz Parmesan, grated, plus extra to sprinkle

a handful of fresh parsley, finely chopped

salt and freshly ground black pepper

for the tomato sauce

2 tbsp extra virgin olive oil

1 small onion, finely chopped

400g can chopped plum tomatoes

It is common in Italy to stuff vegetables such as courgettes (zucchini). Traditionally this is done to enrich vegetables that are in season and make them into a substantial meal for the family. Typical leftovers of cheese, bread and salami are used, while minced (ground) meat and vegetarian fillings are common. This dish is the favourite comfort food of my partner, Liz, whose mum would often make it for her. Liz now makes this for the family and it is indeed yummy and satisfying.

For the sauce, heat the extra virgin olive oil in a pan, add the onion and sweat on a medium heat until softened. Add the tomatoes and season with salt and pepper, then reduce the heat to medium-low, half-cover with a lid and cook for 20 minutes, stirring from time to time.

Preheat the oven to 200°C/400°F/gas mark 6.

Cut the courgettes in half lengthways, scoop out the pulp and put the shells to one side. Heat the extra virgin olive oil in a frying pan, add the garlic and fry on a medium heat for 1 minute, then add the courgette pulp and stir-fry for about 4 minutes, until cooked. Leave to cool.

Combine the minced meats, bread, egg, Parmesan, parsley, cooked courgette pulp, salt and pepper in a bowl – this is best done with your hands. Fill the courgette shells with the mixture.

Pour the tomato sauce into an ovenproof baking dish. Place the filled courgettes on top, drizzle with a little extra virgin olive oil and sprinkle with Parmesan, then cover with foil and bake for 35 minutes. Remove the foil and bake for a further 10 minutes, until the courgettes are cooked through. If the tomato sauce has dried during baking, add a little hot water to the bottom of the dish. Remove from the oven, leave to stand for a couple of minutes, then serve.

650g/1lb 7oz stewing (braising) beef, cut
into chunks

salt and freshly ground black pepper

8 tbsp extra virgin olive oil

a handful of fresh thyme

250ml/9fl oz/generous 1 cup red wine

1 large onion, roughly chopped

2 garlic cloves, crushed

2 celery stalks, roughly chopped

3 carrots, roughly chopped

150g/5½oz cherry tomatoes, halved

2 bay leaves

5 tbsp passata (strained tomatoes)

250ml/9fl oz/generous 1 cup beef or
vegetable stock

Spezzatino di manzo al vino rosso

Red wine beef stew

I love stews and this is one of my favourites, simply cooked with chunks of beef, a few vegetables and red wine. The secret to its rich taste is to cook the beef in the wine before adding the rest of the ingredients, so that the meat absorbs the wine as much as possible. This rich stew, served with runny polenta (cornmeal) or mashed potatoes, is perfect comfort food for all the family.

Rub the beef all over with salt and pepper. Heat the extra virgin olive oil in a large saucepan, add the beef and seal over a medium–high heat for 1–2 minutes on each side.

Stir in the thyme and cook until all the liquid the beef has exuded (unless you are using aged meat) has evaporated. Add the wine, cover with a lid and cook for 5 minutes. Add all the vegetables and bay leaves and season lightly, then add the passata and stock. Bring to the boil, then reduce the heat to low. Cover and cook for about 1 hour 20 minutes, or until the beef is tender and cooked through.

1kg/2lb 4oz stewing pork, cut into chunks

salt and freshly ground black pepper

a little plain (all-purpose) flour

5 tbsp extra virgin olive oil

2 onions, thinly sliced

150g/5½oz baby carrots, peeled

1 celery stalk, roughly chopped

3 fresh sage leaves

100ml/3½fl oz/⅓ cup dry white wine

800ml/1 pint 7fl oz/generous 3 cups hot
vegetable stock (from powder or home-made)

500g/1lb 2oz waxy potatoes, peeled, cut into
chunks

200g/7oz podded fresh or frozen peas

Spezzatino di maiale con patate e piselli

Pork stew with potatoes and peas

This is a simple stew to prepare; however, once you start adding the stock, keep a close eye on it – you don't want to boil the meat. You can substitute stewing lamb for the pork, if you prefer.

Season the pork with salt and pepper and dust with flour. Heat the extra virgin olive oil in a large saucepan, add the onions, carrots, celery and sage leaves and fry on a medium heat, stirring from time to time to prevent the vegetables from burning or sticking, until the onions and celery soften.

Stir in the floured pork and seal for 1–2 minutes on each side. Add the wine and cook until evaporated. Reduce the heat, cover with a lid and cook for 5 minutes. Pour in 2 ladlefuls of hot stock and cook for 45 minutes, adding more stock when necessary.

Stir in the potatoes, with more stock if necessary, cover with a lid and cook for a further 20 minutes. Five minutes before the end of the cooking time, stir in the peas, making sure the potatoes don't break up. Season if necessary and serve.

Cannellini con puntine di maiale

Cannellini beans with spare ribs

- -

SERVES 4

350g/12oz dried cannellini beans, soaked in water overnight

5 tbsp extra virgin olive oil

800g/1lb 12oz pork spare ribs

4 bay leaves

leaves from 1 fresh rosemary stem

6 fresh sage leaves

salt and freshly ground black pepper

1 onion, finely chopped

1 garlic clove, finely chopped

500g/1lb 2oz passata (strained tomatoes)

a handful of fresh parsley, finely chopped, to garnish (optional)

bruschetta, to serve (see page 75)

- -

This rustic dish, traditionally cooked with pigs' trotters and other parts of the pig as well as pieces of lard, was a favourite during winter in most rural regions of Italy. These days, for health reasons, lard and some parts of the pig are not used (except perhaps by traditionalists), and have been replaced by spare ribs, which are equally delicious and less fatty. This dish reminds me of comfort food at home, bringing warmth and cheer to dull, dreary winter days. We would accompany it with bruschetta and the slight charcoaled aroma filled our kitchen and made me ravenous. It was my job to rub the garlic over the bread and drizzle it with the extra virgin olive oil. Whenever I cook a bean dish such as this one, bruschetta is a must and the smell never ceases to amaze me. It is during dark winter evenings that I love to place dried beans to soak in water in preparation for, and anticipation of, the next day's meal.

Drain the beans, then put them into a large saucepan with enough water to cover – about 1.8 litres/3$\frac{1}{4}$ pints/scant 2 quarts. Half-cover with a lid and bring to the boil, then reduce the heat to medium and simmer for 50 minutes, until tender.

Meanwhile, heat the extra virgin olive oil in a large, shallow pan. Add the ribs, bay leaves, rosemary, sage, salt and pepper and seal the ribs over a medium–high heat for 1–2 minutes on each side. Remove them and set aside. Reduce the heat to medium, add the onion and garlic to the pan and sweat for a couple of minutes. Add the passata, 250ml/9fl oz/generous 1 cup hot water and some salt and simmer for 5 minutes. Return the ribs to the pan and cook on a low heat for about 45 minutes, until the meat begins to become detached from the bone. Remove the ribs again and keep warm.

Drain the cooked beans and add to the tomato sauce, then simmer gently for 5 minutes. Remove from the heat and serve with the spare ribs. Garnish with parsley, if desired, and serve with bruschetta.

Salsicce fatte in casa con salsa piccante

Home-made sausages with a spicy sauce

MAKES ABOUT 10 SAUSAGES, EACH ABOUT 60G/2¹⁄₄OZ

450g/1lb minced (ground) pork, at room temperature

20g/³⁄₄oz rocket (arugula), finely chopped

1¹⁄₂ tsp salt

40ml/1¹⁄₂fl oz/scant 3 tbsp dry white wine, at room temperature

1 tsp fennel seeds (optional)

50g/1³⁄₄oz hard mozzarella, cut into small cubes

5 tbsp extra virgin olive oil

for the sauce

2 tsp capers, finely chopped

¹⁄₂ red chilli (chile), finely chopped

1 red onion, finely chopped

1 white onion, finely chopped

1 red (bell) pepper, deseeded and finely chopped

salt

As a little boy I never remember buying sausages from a shop. It was normal for everyone to make their own at home, especially at the time of the killing of the pig, when sausages were in abundance. My sister Adriana and I often make our own sausage, getting the children involved – they love to shape them. I serve them with a spicy sauce; however, for children (unless your's like spicy food) I make a simple tomato sauce. I urge you to buy the best organic minced (ground) pork you can get.

Combine the minced pork, rocket, salt, wine and fennel seeds, if using. Divide into 10 portions. Press a few cubes of mozzarella into the centre of each portion, then roll the meat around the cheese and form it into a sausage shape. Ensure the mozzarella is well enclosed.

Heat the extra virgin olive oil in a large frying pan. Add the sausages and fry to seal on both sides, then cook on a gentle heat, turning from time to time, for about 10 minutes. Increase the heat and cook until golden. Remove the sausages and set aside.

To make the sauce, sauté the capers and chilli in the same frying pan for 1 minute. Add the onions and sweat for 1 minute. Stir in the red pepper and add salt to taste. Add 250ml/9fl oz/generous 1 cup water and bring to the boil, then lower the heat and simmer for 30 minutes.

Add the sausages and continue to cook for 5 minutes, until the sausages are cooked and heated through. Serve immediately with lots of good bread.

Lenticchie con salsicce

Lentils stewed with sausages

SERVES 4

350g/12oz small brown lentils

4 tbsp extra virgin olive oil

1 onion, finely chopped

1 bay leaf

2 fresh sage leaves

1 celery stalk, finely chopped

1 large carrot, finely chopped

8 pork sausages

1.5 litres/2½ pints/1½ quarts vegetable stock
(from powder or home-made)

1 large potato, peeled and finely chopped

1 tbsp tomato purée (paste)

When I was a boy, lentils had to be thoroughly checked for impurities and were soaked overnight. These days it is not necessary to do either; however, I always rinse them first in case a small stone is lurking, and for this recipe I usually soak them for a couple of hours – if you don't soak them, you may find you need to cook them for longer. Lentils and sausages are a great combination and this dish is a simple, one-pot winter warmer that is both filling and nutritious. In Italy, for New Year, lentils are cooked in a similar way and served with *cotecchino* or *zampone*, which is a huge pork sausage usually sold in vacuum packs and cooked separately in boiling water. For maximum flavour buy the smaller variety of brown lentils and, of course, good pork sausages from a trusted butcher. This is delicious served with mashed potato, especially for kids, or with good country bread.

Wash the lentils, discarding any impurities, and leave to soak in fresh cold water for about 2 hours.

Heat the extra virgin olive oil in a large saucepan, add the onion, bay leaf, sage, celery and carrot and stir-fry for a couple of minutes. Add the sausages and cook, turning, to seal all over.

Drain the lentils and add to the pan with the vegetable stock and potato. Bring to the boil, lower the heat, cover with a lid and simmer gently for about 35 minutes, until the lentils are tender.

About 10 minutes before the end of cooking time, stir in the tomato purée. Remove the pan from the heat and serve.

Parmigiana di bietole

Swiss chard Parmigiana

SERVES 4

700g/1lb 9oz Swiss chard

1/2 tbsp plain (all-purpose) flour, plus extra, to dust

3 eggs

6 tbsp freshly grated Parmesan, plus extra to serve

salt and freshly ground black pepper

olive oil, to fry

100g/3^{1}/$_{2}$oz hard mozzarella, cut into small cubes

a few basil leaves

for the tomato sauce

3 tbsp extra virgin olive oil

1 small onion, finely chopped

1^{1}/$_{2}$ x400g cans chopped plum tomatoes

6 fresh basil leaves

a pinch of salt

Originally, Parmigiana was made with aubergines (eggplant) and although the name suggests it comes from 'Parma', the dish claims to be from Campania and Sicily. I love this dish, which I was literally brought up on, and I also make it with courgettes (zucchini). Recently my sister Adriana made it with Swiss chard, a spinach-type vegetable that's slightly bitter when raw, but delicious once cooked. It's a shame Swiss chard is not popular in this country, but it can be found at the market during late summer and autumn. When I was a young boy, the Parmigiana would be served as a side dish and it amazes me now how we could eat this along with a starter of pasta *and* a main course! When I make it, it is usually a main course, served with good bread, to mop up the sauce, and a green salad. Although only the stalks are used for this recipe, don't throw away the green leaves – boil them for a minute or two, then drain and serve with a drizzle of extra virgin olive oil (you could serve this as an accompaniment to the Parmigiana).

For the tomato sauce, heat the extra virgin olive oil in a saucepan, add the onion and sweat on a medium heat until softened. Reduce the heat to low, then add the tomatoes, basil leaves and salt and simmer for 25 minutes, stirring from time to time. Should the sauce appear dry, add a little hot water.

Preheat the oven to 200°C/400°F/gas mark 6.

You want the white stalks and only the tender inner leaves of the Swiss chard. (The discarded harder green leaves can be used in another recipe or cooked as above.) Wash well and dry, then dust with flour. Beat the eggs, stir in 2 tbsp grated Parmesan, the 1/2 tbsp flour and a pinch of salt and pepper. Dip the chard in the beaten egg. Pour enough olive oil in a large frying pan to cover the base generously, then place over a medium–high heat. When hot, fry the chard on both sides until golden. Remove and drain on kitchen towel.

Line a 20 x 22cm/8 x 8^{1}/$_{2}$-inch ovenproof dish with some of the tomato sauce, then arrange a layer of the chard on top, followed by some of the mozzarella, Parmesan and basil leaves. Continue layering like this until you have used up all the ingredients, finishing with a cheese topping.

Bake for about 35 minutes, until golden brown. Switch off the oven and leave the Parmigiana to settle in the oven for 10 minutes before serving sprinkled with extra grated Parmesan.

Pranzo Domenicale

Sunday
Lunch

In Italy, Sunday is still considered an important day for religion, family and food. It's the one day when most people don't work and all the family reunites, usually around the dining table of mamma or nonna. When I was a child, it was the day you wore your 'Sunday best', and I suppose this is still true in smaller towns and villages. I love the atmosphere on Sunday in Italy – the church bells ring and, as Mass ends, the square fills with people, young and old, all immaculately dressed. Some go to the cafés for an aperitivo, some to buy pastries.

When I was a child, my parents, sisters, aunts, uncles and cousins would get together at my grandfather's house for Sunday lunch. He had a big table that would somehow accommodate all of us, up to 25 people. We would all contribute to lunch; my mother brought fresh pasta, my zia Maria meat ragù, and perhaps one of my sisters a dessert. If my father had been hunting, we'd have rabbit or quail, which he would prepare with my grandfather. It was always noisy, with the children laughing and playing, the dogs and cats waiting under the table for scraps, and the adults discussing the food – where it came from (my father's favourite topic), how a dish was cooked, and arguments about whether it should contain this herb or that. It was fun for me to get together with all my cousins, and now Sunday lunch brings back fond memories of family life in my childhood, and how food was a great part of it.

Sunday lunch might not be as noisy these days, and we might not consume as many courses as we did, but it's good to be together, cook together and share a roast or baked pasta dish. Sometimes my sister Adriana and her sons and my good friend Paolo (who is like one of the family) join us, or perhaps my elder daughter visits with her children, and then it does become noisy!

During the autumn, we often go to the forest to forage for mushrooms. The girls love it, and Olivia can spot a porcino before I do. When we have collected enough, we sometimes enjoy a mushroom risotto in the open; it's a special way of spending Sunday – with family, food and nature.

SERVES 4

5 tbsp extra virgin olive oil

1 small onion, finely chopped

2 bay leaves

500g/1lb 2oz beef topside (top round), cut into medium chunks

500g/1lb 2oz pork spare ribs

200g/7oz Italian pork sausages

2 tbsp tomato purée (paste) diluted in 100ml/3$\frac{1}{2}$fl oz/$\frac{1}{3}$ cup red wine

3 x 400g cans chopped plum tomatoes

salt and freshly ground black pepper

a handful of fresh basil leaves

30g/1oz Parmesan, grated

Il ragù di famiglia
My family's meat ragù

This has to be my favourite dish and is reminiscent of my childhood Sunday lunches. Traditionally, meat ragù was slow-cooked in terracotta pots for up to 12 hours. It may seem absurd, but believe me the taste was amazing. My zia Maria was the queen of ragù in our family and each week she would meticulously begin to prepare it the day before, leaving it to cook very gently until late at night, then recommence on Sunday morning, until all the family reunited at my grandfather's house. The tomato sauce was used to dress the home-made ricci pasta and the meat was served as a main course. This dish is still popular for Sunday lunch in most southern Italian families and I certainly like to make it when all the family comes to visit. Of course, the cooking time is greatly reduced. My sister Adriana recently gave me a tip to add chopped Parmesan to the sauce for even more flavour.

Heat the extra virgin olive oil in a saucepan, add the onion and bay leaves and sweat over a medium heat until the onion has softened slightly. Add the beef, ribs and sausages and fry for a few minutes, turning, to brown well.

Stir in the diluted tomato purée and allow to evaporate slightly. Add the tomatoes, salt, pepper, basil and Parmesan and stir well. Bring to the boil, then reduce the heat to low, cover with a lid and cook for 2 hours, checking and stirring from time to time.

Remove from the heat and serve as suggested in the introduction, with pasta or on its own with lots of good bread to mop up the tomato sauce.

Carre' d'agnello con carciofini

Rack of lamb with artichokes and sun-blushed tomatoes

SERVES 4

4 large spring onions (scallions)

1kg/2lb 4oz rack of lamb

salt and freshly ground black pepper

85g/3oz prosciutto, roughly sliced

100ml/3$\frac{1}{2}$fl oz/$\frac{1}{3}$ cup extra virgin olive oil

leaves from 2 sprigs of fresh thyme

250g/9oz preserved artichoke hearts

250g/9oz sun-blushed tomatoes

This is a different way of cooking a roast rack of lamb – the flavours of the prosciutto, preserved artichokes and sun-blushed tomatoes really enhance the meat. It is simple to prepare and perfect to impress the family on a Sunday

Preheat the oven to 200°C/400°F/gas mark 6.

Cut the white parts off most of the spring onions and thinly slice them. Cut the remaining whole spring onions and green parts in half or into long slices, depending on their thickness.

Rub the rack of lamb all over with salt and pepper. Place the strips of prosciutto between the bones followed by the long spring onion slices and halves. Place in a roasting tin (pan) and drizzle with 4 tbsp extra virgin olive oil, rubbing it well in all over. Place in the oven for 30–40 minutes, or until cooked through.

Meanwhile, heat the remaining olive oil in a small pan, add the sliced white parts of the spring onions and sweat for a couple of minutes on a medium heat. Add the thyme, artichokes and tomatoes and cook for a further 2 minutes. About 10 minutes before the lamb is ready, add the vegetables to the roasting tin (pan) and return to the oven to finish cooking.

Lasagne agli asparagi

Lasagne with asparagus

- - - - - - - - - - - - - - - - - - -

SERVES 6

1kg/2lb 4oz asparagus, trimmed
butter, to grease
300g/10^1/$_2$oz dried lasagne sheets
(about 15 sheets)
100g/3^1/$_2$oz cooked ham, roughly chopped
60g/2^1/$_4$oz Parmesan, grated

for the white sauce

60g/2^1/$_4$oz/4 tbsp butter
60g/2^1/$_4$oz/4 tbsp plain (all-purpose) flour
800ml/1 pint 7fl oz/generous 3 cups milk
salt and freshly ground black pepper
2 tsp freshly grated Parmesan

- - - - - - - - - - - - - - - - - - -

The traditional lasagne that is known all over the world comes from Emilia Romagna, where it is commonly eaten for Sunday lunch. The rest of Italy also has its adaptations. This is a contemporary version made with fresh, light ingredients, and is ideal for spring, when asparagus is in season. I make it for my daughter Olivia – she loves asparagus. It can be served as a *primo* (first course), as Italians would, or as a main course, depending on how hungry you are.

Remove the tip from each asparagus stalk and chop the stalks. Bring a large saucepan of lightly salted water to the boil. Add the stalks and tips and cook for 5 minutes, until tender but not overcooked. Drain, then put the tips on a flat plate. Put the stalks in a blender and liquidize. Set both aside.

To make the white sauce, melt the butter in a saucepan, stir in the flour and, using a hand whisk, whisk to a smooth paste, then add a little of the milk and stir. Gradually add the remaining milk, stirring all the time, until it begins to thicken to a creamy consistency. Remove from the heat, add salt, pepper, Parmesan and the liquidized asparagus stalks, and mix well.

Preheat the oven to 200°C/400°F/gas mark 6. Lightly grease a 28 x 22cm/11 x 8^1/$_2$-inch ovenproof dish with butter. Spread a little of the asparagus sauce on the bottom of the dish. Arrange a layer of lasagne sheets on top, followed by some more sauce, then a layer of asparagus tips. Scatter on some of the ham, then sprinkle on some of the Parmesan and a little pepper. Continue layering like this until you have used up all the ingredients, ending with the asparagus sauce topped with Parmesan.

Cover with foil and bake for about 35 minutes, until golden. Ten minutes before the end of the cooking time, remove the foil.

Coniglio all'agrodolce

Marinated rabbit with olives, capers and pine kernels

SERVES 4

1.2kg/2lb 11oz rabbit chunks, washed under cold running water and dried

plain (all-purpose) flour, to dust

6 tbsp extra virgin olive oil

1 onion, thinly sliced

140g/5oz bacon, finely chopped

4 bay leaves

1 celery heart, thinly sliced

50g/1¾oz raisins, soaked in a little warm water and drained

2 tbsp capers

2 tbsp pine kernels

85g/3oz pitted green olives

3 tbsp red wine vinegar

1 tsp caster (superfine) sugar

salt and freshly ground black pepper

for the marinade

200ml/7fl oz/scant 1 cup red wine

1 onion, thinly sliced

2 bay leaves

20 black peppercorns

Rabbit was always a popular choice for Sunday lunch at home in Italy. My father and grandfather used to hunt and, along with game birds, they would bring home rabbits. My father insisted on cooking what he hunted and my mother was not allowed to do the cleaning and preparing (to be honest, she was pleased). This was always quite a lengthy procedure – after the rabbits had been skinned, they would be soaked in a solution of water and lemon for 24 hours to rid them of impurities, then rinsed a few times and dried, ready to be cooked. We would have them simply roasted with lots of garlic and rosemary, but also as *agrodolce* (sweet and sour) to enhance the taste of the slightly gamey flesh of the rabbit. I still like to cook rabbit in England and my older son, Christopher, has loved it since he was a child, so when he comes to visit I cook it for him. If you can't find rabbit, substitute chicken or guinea fowl and remove the skin before marinating.

Combine all the ingredients for the marinade in a small saucepan, bring to the boil and cook for 1 minute. Remove from the heat and leave to cool. Put the rabbit in a bowl, pour over the marinade, cover and refrigerate for at least 6 hours, or overnight.

Remove the rabbit from the marinade and pat dry on kitchen towel. Dust in flour, then shake off any excess. Heat 4 tbsp extra virgin olive oil in a large saucepan over a medium–high heat, add the rabbit and cook for 1–2 minutes on each side to seal all over. Remove the rabbit and set aside. Reduce the heat to medium and pour the remaining olive oil into the saucepan. Add the onion, bacon and bay leaves and sweat for a couple of minutes. Add the celery, raisins, capers, pine kernels and olives and sweat for a further couple of minutes.

Meanwhile, heat the vinegar and sugar together in a small saucepan until the sugar dissolves. Remove from the heat and set aside. Return the rabbit to the large saucepan and pour the vinegar mixture over it, then add salt and pepper to taste, cover with a lid and cook on a medium–low heat for 5 minutes. Gradually add 400ml/14floz/1¾ cups hot water (you may need a little more or less) and cook for about 30 minutes, until the rabbit is tender. The result is a dense sauce. Serve immediately with lots of good country bread.

1 small head of garlic, cloves separated
but unpeeled

5 large fresh sage leaves, finely chopped

leaves from 2 fresh rosemary stems,
finely chopped

a handful of fresh mint, finely chopped

a handful of marjoram leaves, finely chopped

juice of 1 lemon (keep the lemon halves)

100g/3$\frac{1}{2}$oz/scant $\frac{1}{2}$ cup butter, softened

salt and freshly ground black pepper

1 x 1.5kg/3lb 5oz chicken

4 carrots, halved lengthways

extra virgin olive oil, to drizzle

6 tbsp dry white wine

175ml/6fl oz/$\frac{3}{4}$ cup vegetable stock
(from powder or homemade)

Pollo arrosto con aglio, limone ed erbe

Roast chicken with garlic, lemon and herbs

I love to have a traditional roast chicken for Sunday lunch, and to make it more moist I spread a paste of roasted garlic and herbs over the flesh. In Italy we used to keep chickens. They were free to roam about the yard and my mum would feed them well. In return, their eggs and meat were delicious. I urge you to buy the best organic free-range chicken you can – it really makes a difference. This is great with Adriana's roast potatoes (see page 169).

Preheat the oven to 220°C/425°F/gas mark 7. Place the garlic cloves on a baking sheet and roast for about 15 minutes, until soft. With the help of a tea towel, remove the skins while still warm. Place the softened garlic in a small bowl with the chopped herbs, lemon juice, butter, salt and pepper. Mix well until you obtain a smooth, but not runny, paste.

Starting at the neck end, carefully ease the skin of the chicken away from the breast, taking care not to tear the delicate skin. Using your fingers, spread the paste evenly under the skin all over the breast, then gently pat the skin to even out the paste. Fill the cavity of the chicken with the lemon halves.

Line the bottom of a roasting pan with the carrots, arranging them in 2 lines like a railway track. Place the chicken on top of the carrots – this will prevent the bird from sticking to the tin. Season the chicken with salt and pepper and drizzle with olive oil, rubbing it well all over. Pour in the wine and stock and cover the tin with foil.

Roast for about 1$\frac{1}{2}$ hours, removing the foil 20 minutes before the end of cooking time, until the chicken is cooked through. Pierce the thickest part of the flesh with a skewer; if the juices run clear it is cooked, but any sign of pink and it needs longer. Remove from the oven and leave to rest for 10 minutes before carving.

Triglie al prosciutto

Red mullet filled with prosciutto

- -

SERVES 6

6 x 200g/7oz red mullet (or red snapper),
scaled, gutted and cleaned

olive oil, to grease

dried breadcrumbs, to coat

4 fresh sage leaves, finely chopped

2 egg whites

12 slices of prosciutto

for the marinade

juice of 2 lemons

1 tsp finely grated unwaxed lemon zest

4 tbsp extra virgin olive oil

salt and freshly ground black pepper

- -

The red mullet is a much-favoured Mediterranean fish. They were highly prized in ancient Roman times, when they were reared in ponds and treated like pets, and it is said some were even sold for their weight in silver! I remember when the fishmonger had local red mullet for sale, word got around and people would race to be first in the queue. We used to enjoy them simply fried and they were always a delicious treat, so I had to include a recipe for this wonderfully delicate fish in this book. Although it is simple enough to make, they take a while to prepare, which is why I've kept them for Sunday lunch. Ask your fishmonger to clean and gut them and I leave it to you to decide whether you want to keep the heads intact – I do.

Put the fish in a shallow non-reactive baking dish. Combine all the ingredients for the marinade in a bowl. Pour over the fish, cover and leave for a couple of hours in the fridge.

When ready to cook, preheat the oven to 190°C/375°F/gas mark 5. Lightly grease a baking sheet with olive oil.

Mix the breadcrumbs with the sage and salt and pepper to taste. Gently whisk the egg whites with a fork. Drain the fish from the marinade. Place 2 slices of prosciutto in the cavity of each fish, then press the edges together to close securely. Dip in the egg whites, then coat in the breadcrumbs, pressing well so they stick to the fish.

Carefully put the filled fish on the baking sheet. Pour the marinade in, around the sides of the baking sheet (not over the fish), and bake for 12–15 minutes, or until golden and cooked. Remove from the oven, leave to rest for a couple of minutes, then serve.

Risotto ai funghi

Risotto with mushrooms

- - - - - - - - - - - - - - - - - -

SERVES 4

1.5 litres/2¹/₂ pints/1¹/₂ quarts good
vegetable stock

4 tbsp extra virgin olive oil

1 small onion, finely chopped

1 celery stalk, finely chopped

375g/13oz/scant 2 cups arborio rice

175ml/6fl oz/³/₄ cup dry white wine

200g/7oz mixed mushrooms, wild or cultivated,
roughly chopped (if you are using cultivated
mushrooms add 10g/³/₄oz dried porcini,
regenerated in water – keep the water)

50g/1³/₄oz/4 tbsp butter

50g/1³/₄oz Parmesan, grated

salt and freshly ground black pepper

- - - - - - - - - - - - - - - - - -

England has always been a joy for me – but never more so than when I discovered the many forests and woods full of fungi. During autumn I like to go to the woods and forage; they are a haven of peace and where I feel at my best. I have passed my passion on to my children and, whenever we can at the weekends, we go on mushroom hunts, with both girls competing with each other as to who can find the first porcini and who can fill their basket the fastest. Sometimes, as a treat, I bring the camping stove and we end the day with a mushroom feast, making a wonderful risotto. If you don't have wild mushrooms, use cultivated ones plus dried porcini.

Heat the extra virgin olive oil in a medium, heavy-based saucepan. Add the onion and celery and sweat until softened. Stir in the rice with a wooden spoon and coat each grain with the oil. Add the wine and allow to evaporate. Stir in the mushrooms and regenerated porcini, if using, adding a couple of tablespoons of the water. Add a couple of ladles of hot stock and, stirring continuously, cook until the stock is absorbed. Add more stock and repeat. Continue adding stock in this way, cooking and stirring, for about 20 minutes, until the rice is cooked – it should be soft on the outside but al dente on the inside.

Remove from the heat and, with a wooden spoon, beat in the butter and Parmesan until the risotto has a creamy consistency. Check for seasoning and, if necessary, add some salt and pepper. Leave to rest for 1 minute, then serve.

500ml/18fl oz/generous 2 cups hot milk
(not boiling)

$1/2$ vanilla pod (cut lengthways) or $1/2$ tsp
finely grated unwaxed lemon zest

6 egg yolks

150g/5$1/2$oz/$3/4$ cup caster
(superfine) sugar

50g/1$3/4$oz/$1/3$ cup plain
(all-purpose) flour, sifted

1 generous tbsp unsweetened
cocoa powder, sifted

200g/7oz savoiardi biscuits

200ml/7fl oz/scant 1 cup Marsala

- - - - - - - - - - - - - - - - - - - -

Zuppa inglese

Italian trifle

This is not an English soup, as the title suggests, but an Italian trifle. I am not sure where this recipe originates from, but it is suggested that the cooks of the Dukes of Este in Ferrara tried to recreate the English trifle after visits to England. The word *'zuppa'* (soup) in Italian cooking refers to both sweet and savoury dishes. The trifle is traditionally made with vanilla and chocolate *crema pasticciera* (custard) and *alchermes* (an aromatic, herb-infused, red-coloured liqueur); I have used Marsala, a traditional Sicilian fortified sweet wine, instead. If you can't find savoiardi biscuits, use sponge boudoir fingers. This recipe can be made the day before you plan to eat and stored in the fridge, and is a lovely family dessert for a Sunday lunch.

Put the milk in a jug, drop in the vanilla pod or lemon zest and leave to infuse. Meanwhile, whisk together the egg yolks and sugar for about 5 minutes, until the sugar has dissolved and the mixture is smooth and creamy. Add the flour and continue to whisk until well amalgamated. Strain the milk through a sieve, then whisk it into the egg mixture. Transfer to a pan and place on a low heat, stirring continuously, until it thickens. Pour half the custard into a bowl and add the cocoa powder, then whisk well, until amalgamated. Leave the 2 custards to cool.

Dip the savoiardi biscuits into the Marsala and use to line a serving bowl. Spoon in a layer of vanilla custard, then lay on more savoiardi biscuits, then chocolate custard. Continue layering, finishing with the chocolate custard, until you have used all the ingredients. Place in the fridge until required. Serve.

FESTE

Special Occasions

Italians don't need a special occasion to celebrate; as long as the table is laid and good food is prepared, every meal is a feast. However, certain times are deemed important: Christmas, Easter, birthdays, saints' days (each town and village in Italy has one), first communion and christenings, to name just a few. Preparations begin at least two days in advance, even earlier for Christmas and Easter. My father used to secure the best fish for Christmas Eve or lamb or baby goat for Easter. Our kitchen was buzzing with activity leading up to the festivities, with my mother, grandmother, zia Maria, sisters and cousins rolling out pasta, stirring pots of ragù, preparing biscuits and making desserts.

On these occasions we ate many courses, and in traditional Italian families today it is still usual to serve an array of antipasto dishes (which would normally be more than enough for one meal), followed by a special pasta dish – in our house, this was normally a pasta al forno (baked pasta), while in northern Italy filled pasta such as ravioli, tortellini or cappellacci might be served. Then the main course would be meat or fish prepared in a special way, with vegetables and salads. To finish the meal, some cheese, fruit and, of course, a dessert or even lots of sweet treats would be served, as is traditional at Christmas.

Not all occasions require so many courses; sometimes just one dish is prepared. For example, for Carnevale (the week before Lent begins), it is usual to make sweet treats such as chiacchere (small fried pastries) or zeppole (doughnuts). These were traditionally made at home, but can now be bought in pasticcierie, and each region has its own way of making them. On the feast day of our village each year, we celebrate the saint (Santa Trofimena) with a plate of ndundari (ricotta dumplings with tomato sauce).

When I was growing up, your onomoastico (name day) counted more than your birthday. On the day of San Gennaro on 19th September I was always made a fuss of and my mother would make me a special cake. Gradually this has changed, and birthdays have taken over from name days, but some families still make birthday cakes at home and celebrate with the family.

4 slices of Parma ham

4 slices of mortadella

4 slices of capocollo (cured
pork shoulder)

8 slices of Milano salame

250g/9oz buffalo mozzarella, roughly
sliced

a handful of green and black olives

a selection of preserved vegetables
such as (bell) peppers, aubergines
(eggplants), artichokes, sun-dried
tomatoes and mushrooms

grissini, bruschetta, focaccia and
country bread, to serve

Antipasto tradizionale

Classic antipasto

This classic Italian starter is traditionally served on special occasions such as Christmas. In rural Italy years ago every family had a pig, which was killed each year so that different cuts of cured meat would be available in the larder (pantry). The family also made numerous jars of preserved vegetables and their own cheese. All this produce would be carefully assembled to be enjoyed as an antipasto or starter. Nowadays, all you need is a trip to the supermarket or Italian deli to find these delicacies. Arrange them on big platters in the middle of the table and let everyone help themselves. Make sure you have plenty of good bread and grissini. You can also enhance this course by making some bruschetta (see page 132).

Arrange the meats, mozzarella, olives and preserves on a large platter. Serve with grissini, bruschetta, focaccia and country bread.

Bruschetta caprese

Bruschetta with tomatoes, mozzarella and olives

SERVES 4

4 slices of good country bread

1 large garlic clove, peeled

4 tbsp extra virgin olive oil

12 cherry tomatoes, quartered

1 ball of buffalo mozzarella, roughly torn

12 pitted black olives

a pinch of dried oregano

salt

8 fresh basil leaves

Bruschetta was always made with leftover bread, which was toasted in the oven, then rubbed with garlic, anointed with olive oil and finished with whatever toppings were in season. We enjoyed this classic Mediterranean version during the summer. Nowadays, of course, bruschetta is eaten all year round and served in restaurants as a starter. I make it at home, especially when I'm barbecuing meat; the toasted bread with the slight smokiness is delicious. I usually serve it as a starter before the meat is cooked, and no sooner is a plate of it put in the centre of the table than it magically disappears and I get requests for more. It is ideal for large groups of people at parties; it looks lovely on a big platter and taste delicious.

Grill the bread, then immediately rub the garlic over one side and drizzle with half the extra virgin olive oil.

Combine the tomatoes, mozzarella, olives, oregano and salt in a bowl. Divide between the grilled bread, drizzle with the remaining olive oil and top with basil leaves. Serve.

Raviolini in brodo

Small ravioli in broth

SERVES 4–6

1 quantity of beef broth (see page 20)
1 quantity of fresh pasta (see page 32)
plain (all-purpose) flour, to dust
Parmesan, grated, to serve

for the filling
100g/3½oz cold roast beef
1 tbsp fresh thyme leaves, finely chopped
35g/1¼oz Parmesan, grated
salt and freshly ground black pepper, to taste
2 tbsp dry white wine
1 egg

A small, meat-filled pasta in a good home-made broth is traditionally served during Christmas lunch in most households throughout northern Italy. This recipe was given to me by my wife Liz, whose mother, aunt and grandmother would make it for that special occasion. As a little girl, she would often help her mum on Christmas Eve by rolling the pasta and placing dollops of filling on it (as well as tasting them!), and at the end she had to count the ravioli in order to make sure that there were enough for all the family and guests to eat on Christmas Day. These small ravioli are typically served with a broth, but you can make larger ones, which are normally eaten in a butter and sage sauce or with truffle.

Make the beef broth according to the recipe on page 20. Strain the broth and use the meat and vegetables for another meal.

Make the fresh pasta according to the recipe on page 32. Wrap the dough in clingfilm (plastic wrap) and place in the fridge until ready to use.

For the filling, place the beef in a food processor and whizz until finely chopped. Transfer to a bowl and combine with the rest of the ingredients. Set aside.

Roll out the pasta in a pasta machine until it is wafer thin (see page 32). Place on a work surface lightly dusted with flour and, using a 3cm/1-inch round cutter, cut out circles. Place a little filling on each one, fold in half and press the edges down well with your fingertips to seal.

Place the beef broth in a large saucepan and bring to the boil, then gently drop in the raviolini and cook for about 3 minutes, until al dente. Remove from the heat and serve with the broth, with a sprinkling of freshly grated Parmesan.

Pasta al forno tradizionale

Special baked pasta

- -

SERVES 6

500g/1lb 2oz rigatoni

100g/3½oz Parmesan, grated,
plus extra to sprinkle

70g/2½oz salami, sliced and chopped

3 eggs, hard-boiled and quartered

300g/10½oz mozzarella, cubed

200g/7oz ricotta

for the meatballs

250g/9oz minced (ground) beef

250g/9oz minced (ground) pork

100g/3½oz stale bread, crusts removed,
softened in a little milk, then drained

40g/1½oz Parmesan, grated

1 garlic clove, finely chopped

1 egg

salt and freshly ground black pepper

plain (all-purpose) flour, to dust

good vegetable or seed oil, to deep-fry

for the tomato sauce

4 tbsp extra virgin olive oil

1 onion, finely chopped

3 x 400g cans chopped plum tomatoes

a handful of fresh basil leaves

- - - - - - - - - - - - - - - - - - - -

This dish was a must for us on special occasions such as Christmas lunch, a wedding or communion feast. *Pasta al forno* is common throughout Italy and each region, village and family has its own version. It would be made the day before the festivities and everyone had their role in the preparation. My zia Maria made the tomato sauce – she claimed to be the best (now I think back, this was true!), my sister Carmelina was in charge of the meatballs, perhaps with the help of another sister, and my mother would make the fresh pasta (as was usual for a feast). Even if I sometimes didn't know what occasion it was, I knew when my family got together to make *Pasta al forno* that an important celebration was imminent. This takes a little time to prepare, but the result is really worthwhile.

For the meatballs, combine the beef, pork, soaked and drained bread, Parmesan, garlic, egg, salt and pepper in a bowl. Shape into small balls the size of cherries. Dust with flour, then shake off any excess. Heat oil for deep-frying in a pan until a small piece of bread dropped in sizzles, then cook the meatballs, in batches if necessary, until golden. Drain on kitchen towel and set aside.

For the sauce, heat the extra virgin olive oil in a saucepan, add the onion and sweat on a medium heat until softened. Add the tomatoes and basil and season to taste. Bring to the boil, then lower the heat, half-cover the pan and simmer gently for 25 minutes. Five minutes before the end of the cooking time, add the cooked meatballs. When cooked, remove from the heat and, using a slotted spoon, lift out the meatballs and set aside on a plate.

Preheat the oven to 200°C/400°F/gas mark 6.

Cook the rigatoni in lightly salted water until al dente, according to the instructions on the packet. Drain and return to the saucepan with half the tomato sauce and half the Parmesan, and stir gently.

Line an ovenproof dish with some of the tomato sauce. Spoon some pasta over the sauce, then a little of the salami, some egg quarters, mozzarella, ricotta, Parmesan and meatballs. Continue layering like this until you have used up all the ingredients, ending with tomato sauce and a sprinkling of Parmesan. Bake for 40 minutes. Leave to rest for a couple of minutes, then serve.

Porchetta

Stuffed rolled pork belly

SERVES 10–12

5kg/11lb pork belly (ask your butcher to remove the ribs and trim the excess fat)

25g/1oz coarse sea salt

freshly ground coarse black pepper

small green leaves from a large handful of fresh thyme

leaves from a large handful of fresh rosemary, roughly chopped

a large handful of fresh sage leaves, roughly chopped

1 tbsp fennel seeds (if you are lucky enough to find wild fennel use it)

8 garlic cloves, finely chopped

2 tbsp extra virgin olive oil

potatoes, peeled and cut into chunks

small carrots, cut into chunks

6 tbsp runny honey

Porchetta to me means a party and I make it during special occasions, when I know hordes of people will drop by. It feeds lots, can be eaten cold and can be stored in the fridge for up to a week. Traditionally in Italy, *porchetta* is a whole piglet filled with lots of fresh herbs and slow-roasted either in a wood oven or even outdoors on a spit. It is made at home, as well as sold ready-made as a takeaway. Since whole piglets are not that easily obtainable, I use pork belly and the result is similar. It is simple to prepare and can be made in advance and eaten cold – a great idea for large gatherings. It's ideal served with preserved vegetables such as Giardiniera (see page 224) and Preserved aubergines (see page 226).

Preheat the oven to 220°C/425°F/Gas 7. Lay the pork belly flat, skin side down. Sprinkle with half the salt and lots of black pepper, rubbing it well into the meat with your fingers. Leave to rest for 10 minutes so that the seasoning settles well into the meat. Sprinkle the herbs, fennel seeds and garlic evenly all over.

You will need 10 pieces of string, each about 30cm/12 inches long. Carefully roll the meat up widthways and tie it very tightly with string in the middle of the joint. Then tie at either end about 1cm/$\frac{1}{2}$ inch from the edge and keep tying along the joint until you have used up all the string. The filling should be well wrapped – if any escapes from the sides, push it in. Using your hands, massage 1 tbsp extra virgin olive oil over the joint, then rub in the remaining salt and some more black pepper.

Grease a large roasting pan with the remaining olive oil and place the pork in it. Roast for 10 minutes, then turn it over. After 15 minutes, reduce the oven temperature to 150°C/300°F/gas mark 2 and cover the pork with foil (if you like the crackling to be very crispy, don't bother with the foil, but remember the *porchetta* needs to be thinly sliced and crispy crackling will make that difficult). Roast for 3 hours.

If cooking the potatoes and carrots, add them to the roasting dish for the final 1$\frac{1}{2}$ hours of cooking.

Remove the joint from the oven and coat with the honey, drizzling some of the juices from the roasting tin over it too. Insert a fork at either side of the joint and lift onto a wooden board. Leave to rest for 5 minutes, then slice and serve hot or cold.

Soffritto Napoletano

Spicy meat stew

SERVES 6–8

500g/1lb 2oz pig's liver

300g/10½oz pig's lung

300g/10½oz pig's heart

2 pig's kidneys

½ pig's spleen

4 tbsp olive oil

200g/7oz pork lard

250ml/9fl oz/generous 1 cup red wine

4 red chillies (chiles), finely chopped

1 red (bell) pepper, roasted, deseeded and finely chopped

5 bay leaves

1 fresh rosemary sprig

a small handful of fresh sage

6 tbsp tomato purée (paste)

1 litre/1¾ pints/4 cups hot vegetable stock

6 large bread rolls, soft crumb pulled out and discarded, or thick slices of rustic bread, oven-baked on a low setting until crispy

extra virgin olive oil, to drizzle

This is not an obvious recipe for a family book, but in my family it was very popular, especially among the men. When I was a boy, the local inns in the village would serve it as a working man's breakfast, presented in a large hollow bread roll, which certainly kept the men going for most of the day. This 400-year-old Neapolitan recipe originates from *cucina povera*, when the poor would wait outside the kitchens of the rich nobles for the discarded innards of the beasts being cooked. They took the innards home to their wives, who came up with this spicy recipe. Many would say that this poor man's dish – *soffritto* – actually tasted better than the rich man's meal.

Wash the liver, lung, heart, kidneys and spleen in cold water and dry them with a cloth, then slice them into small chunks.

Heat the olive oil and lard in a large saucepan. Add the liver, lung, heart, kidneys and spleen and cook, stirring, until everything is well sealed on all sides. Add the wine and allow to evaporate, then stir in the chillies, roasted pepper, bay leaves, rosemary, sage and tomato purée and cook for 5 minutes. Add the hot stock and simmer for about 1 hour, checking from time to time to ensure that the meat isn't sticking, and if necessary adding some more stock. At the end of the cooking time, the stew should have a creamy consistency.

Place the crispy bread rolls or slices on individual plates, fill with the soffritto, drizzle with extra virgin olive oil and serve immediately. Alternatively, serve on slices of baked bread.

Agnello brodettato

Easter lamb

SERVES 4

4 tbsp extra virgin olive oil

1kg/2lb 4oz lamb shoulder, cut into chunks

1 onion, finely chopped

40g/1¹/₂oz prosciutto, roughly chopped

175ml/6fl oz/³/₄ cup dry white wine

2 litres/3¹/₂ pints/2 quarts hot vegetable stock

1 potato, peeled and cut into small chunks

yolks from 2 hard-boiled eggs

1 fresh marjoram stalk

1 tbsp finely chopped fresh parsley

finely grated zest and juice of ¹/₂ small
unwaxed lemon

This is a traditional dish prepared at Easter in most of central and southern Italy, using the new season's spring baby lamb and eggs. Originally it was made with baby goat and raw eggs, in the days when you knew where your eggs came from (probably your own backyard). When I was a child, my family would always celebrate Easter by cooking a baby goat, and sometimes *brodettato*-style (which roughly translates as 'in a broth'). I have added lemon, herbs and hard-boiled egg yolks for a lighter alternative. The sauce is delicate and tasty. Serve with boiled new potatoes and the new season's fresh peas.

Heat the extra virgin olive oil in a large saucepan, add the lamb and brown well all over on a high heat. Reduce the heat to medium, add the onion and prosciutto and stir-fry for 3 minutes. Add the wine and allow to evaporate. Add the hot stock and potato, cover with a lid and cook for 45 minutes, until the lamb is cooked and tender.

Remove the lamb and set aside. Remove the sauce from the heat, stir in the hardboiled egg yolks, herbs and lemon juice and liquidize to a smooth, creamy sauce. Serve immediately with the lamb chunks and a sprinkling of lemon zest.

Fritto misto di pesce

Mixed fried fish

SERVES 4

200g/7oz king prawns (jumbo shrimp),
raw and unpeeled

200g/7oz whitebait

200g/7oz squid (calamari), cleaned
and cut into rings and tentacles

200g/7oz sardines, gutted

grated zest of 2 unwaxed lemons

1 small garlic clove, finely chopped

a handful of fresh parsley, finely chopped

good vegetable or seed oil, to deep-fry

lemon wedges, to serve

for the batter

2 egg yolks

a pinch of salt

200g/7oz/1⅓ cups plain
(all-purpose) flour, sifted

This dish was commonly served during the Christmas Eve feast, when meat was not permitted and the meal consisted of fish and vegetables. A large platter of *fritto misto* was placed in the middle of the table and everyone helped themselves. *Fritto misto* is also popular in restaurants at coastal resorts throughout Italy. The traditional way of making this dish was to simply dust the fish with flour and then fry them. I like a light batter, which works really well with the delicate flavour of the fish. The secret of this recipe is to use really fresh fish.

Place the prawns, whitebait, squid and sardines in a shallow dish and scatter half the lemon zest and all the garlic and parsley over them. Cover and refrigerate for 30 minutes.

To make the batter, whisk the egg yolks in a bowl, then gradually whisk in 40ml/1½fl oz/scant 3 tbsp very cold water and the salt. Gradually fold in the flour, until well amalgamated.

Heat the oil for deep-frying in a large saucepan or deep-fryer until a small piece of bread dropped in sizzles immediately. Remove the fish from the fridge and dip each piece into the batter, then immediately fry a few pieces at a time for a few minutes, until golden and the fish is cooked. Drain on kitchen towel and serve immediately, scattered with the remaining lemon zest, with lemon wedges.

Spiedini di polipo

Skewered octopus

MAKES ABOUT 10 SKEWERS

1kg/2lb 4oz octopus (thawed if frozen)

4 bay leaves

1 fresh rosemary sprig

1/2 tbsp black peppercorns

2 slices of unwaxed lemon zest

olive oil, to grease

150g/5 1/2oz breadcrumbs (whizz stale crustless rustic bread in a food processor)

a handful of fresh parsley, finely chopped

1 fresh thyme sprig, finely chopped

1 fresh marjoram sprig, finely chopped

1 garlic clove, finely chopped

1 large red onion, thickly sliced

salt and freshly ground black pepper

Octopus reminds me of my youth, diving deep down into the sea to collect these amazing sea creatures. The ones I collected lived by the rocks and were slightly grey and smaller than normal, weighing no more than about 400g/14oz each. These smaller ones can be simply cooked with a little extra virgin olive oil in their own juice. The larger ones were found out in the ocean and were caught by fishermen using *luce dei lampari* (oil lamps), which were lit at night to attract the octopus, which would come up to the surface to investigate. The larger octopus has to be cooked in water with some herbs, as in this recipe. These skewers make a great alternative to the usual meat ones and, with the red onion and herby breadcrumbs, are really delicious. They take a little time to prepare, but are well worth the effort when friends come round. They can be served as an antipasto or as part of a selection of dishes at a party. If you have any breadcrumbs left over, put them on a baking tray and bake for a few minutes until golden. Use them to top the skewers just before serving.

Bring a large saucepan of water to the boil. Pick the octopus up by its head and gently dip into the boiling water 3 times. You will notice the tentacles curl up. Discard the boiling water.

Place the octopus in a large clean saucepan with the bay leaves, rosemary, peppercorns and lemon zest and fill with cold water. Bring to the boil, then reduce the heat, partially cover with a lid and simmer gently for 50 minutes or until the octopus is tender. Remove from the heat and leave the octopus in the cooking water to settle for about 30 minutes. Preheat the oven to 190°C/375°F/gas mark 5. Lightly grease a baking tray (sheet) with extra virgin olive oil.

Meanwhile, mix together the breadcrumbs, herbs and garlic in a bowl. Remove the octopus from the pan and drain, then slice into chunks. Thread alternate chunks of octopus and onion slices on to the skewers. Coat the skewers in the breadcrumb mixture. Place on the baking tray, drizzle with some extra virgin olive oil and sprinkle with salt and pepper.

Bake for 5 minutes, then turn the skewers over, add some of the leftover breadcrumb mixture and continue baking until golden. Can be enjoyed warm or cold.

Torta festiva

Celebration cake

butter, to grease

6 eggs

300g/10^1/$_2$oz/1^1/$_2$ cups caster (superfine) sugar

200g/7oz/1^1/$_3$ cups plain (all-purpose) flour, sifted

3 tsp baking powder, sifted

for the filling

750ml/1 pint 6fl oz/3 cups milk

1 vanilla pod

9 egg yolks

300g/10^1/$_2$oz/1^1/$_2$ cups caster (superfine) sugar

75g/2^3/$_4$oz cornflour (cornstarch)

60g/2^1/$_4$ oz good plain (semisweet) chocolate, finely chopped

for the syrup

100ml/3^1/$_2$fl oz/^{1}/$_3$ cup Marsala

40g/1^1/$_2$oz/scant ^{1}/$_4$ cup caster (superfine) sugar

for the decoration

a selection of fruit, such as strawberries, kiwi, blueberries, cherries, raspberries and figs

icing (confectioners') sugar, sifted

This is a typical Italian celebration cake, made for birthdays and other festivities. The sponge, known as *pan di spagna*, is drizzled with a syrup made from water and a sweet liqueur, which makes it very moist. The filling is usually a *crema pasticciera* (custard cream), which is home-made and can be flavoured with vanilla and/or chocolate.

This cake can be decorated as you like; I use fresh fruit, which is quite traditional. However, you can use your imagination and make a cake that is suitable for any member of your family, for any occasion. My sister Adriana is an expert cake maker and decorator and makes this cake for her sons' birthdays, changing the decorations accordingly.

First, make the sponge. Preheat the oven to 180°C/350°F/ gas mark 4. Grease a deep 20cm/8-inch square cake tin (pan), or 3 x 20cm/8-inch round sandwich tins (pans) if you have them, then set aside.

For the sponge, whisk the eggs and sugar together in a bowl until creamy and foamy. Gradually fold in the flour and baking powder. Pour into the cake tin/s and bake for 40 minutes if using a large tin and 15–20 minutes if using small tins.

CONTINUED OVERLEAF...

Check it is done by inserting a wooden skewer, if it comes out clean and dry the sponge is ready. Leave to cool, then tip out of the tin/s. If you have made 1 cake, cut it horizontally into 3 sponges.

For the filling, pour the milk into a small saucepan, add the vanilla pod and heat until the milk reaches boiling point. Meanwhile, whisk the egg yolks and sugar in a bowl until light and fluffy. Add the cornflour and continue to whisk.

Gradually pour the milk into the egg mixture, whisking all the time to prevent lumps forming. Once well amalgamated, pour the mixture back into the pan, place on a medium heat and stir. As soon as it begins to boil, remove from the heat (do this quickly or the cream on the bottom of the pan will burn).

Pour a third of the mixture into another bowl and immediately stir in the chocolate until well amalgamated and the chocolate has melted. You will then have a vanilla filling and a chocolate filling – cover both with clingfilm and leave to cool.

For the syrup, put the Marsala and sugar in a small saucepan with 200ml/7fl oz/scant 1 cup water and cook on a medium heat, stirring, until the sugar has dissolved and the liquid has reduced a little. Leave to cool. Brush each layer of sponge with the syrup.

Spread the first sponge layer with vanilla filling. Add a second layer of sponge and spread with the chocolate filling. Add a third layer of sponge and top with the remaining vanilla filling. Decorate with the fruit and dust with sifted icing sugar.

Chiacchiere

Carnival biscuits

SERVES 4–6

300g/10 ¹/₂ oz/generous 2 cups plain
(all-purpose) flour

70g/2¹/₂ oz/¹/₃ cup caster (superfine) sugar

2 eggs, beaten

100g/3¹/₂oz/scant ¹/₂ cup butter, melted

finely grated zest of 1 unwaxed lemon

5 tsp rum

good vegetable oil, to deep-fry

icing (confectioners') sugar, to dust

These are traditional biscuits made all over Italy for *Carnevale*, the period just before Lent, and are known by various regional names. I enjoy making them each year with my girls – we roll out the pastry with the pasta machine and then cut them out with a pasta cutter, giving the biscuits a decorative curly edge. They are light and delicious and once you start eating one, you don't stop, so it's always worth making lots.

Place the flour on a clean work surface and make a well in the centre. Add the sugar, eggs, butter, lemon zest and rum and mix well to form a smooth dough. Wrap in clingfilm (plastic wrap) and place in the fridge for a couple of hours.

Lightly flour a work surface and roll out the dough in a rectangular shape to a thickness of 3mm/¹/₈ inch. Using a pastry cutter, cut into strips of 2cm/³/₄ inch wide, making a small incision with the cutter in the middle of each strip.

Heat the vegetable oil for deep frying in a large saucepan or deep-fryer until a small piece of bread dropped into it sizzles immediately. Add the chiacchere in batches of a few at a time and fry, turning each one until they are golden brown. Drain on kitchen towel, allow to cool, then sprinkle with some icing sugar.

Frittelle dolci di patate

Potato doughnuts

- - - - - - - - - - - - - - - -

MAKES ABOUT 12

250g/9oz floury potatoes

250g/9oz/1²/₃ cups '00' flour or strong plain (all-purpose bread) flour, plus extra to dust

1 x 7g sachet of dried yeast, dissolved in 2 tbsp lukewarm water

2 eggs

50g/1³/₄oz/¹/₄ cup caster (superfine) sugar, plus extra to dust

50g/1³/₄oz/scant 4 tbsp butter, softened

a pinch of salt

finely grated zest of 1 orange

1 vanilla pod

good vegetable or seed oil, to fry

cinnamon powder, to dust

- - - - - - - - - - - - - - - -

This sweet doughnut made with potato is a recipe from the Amalfi coast, where they are made during *Carnevale,* when people throw parties and eat lots of sweet treats. It is a typical recipe from home and not a dish you'll find in the pastry shops. I remember as a child helping my older sisters to roll the dough out and I couldn't wait for them to be cooked and ready for me to eat. They are lighter and much healthier than the usual shop-bought versions.

Boil the potatoes in their skins for 15–25 minutes, until tender. Cool a little, then remove the skins and mash the potatoes with a ricer.

Place the flour in a large bowl or on a clean work surface, make a well in the centre and add the mashed potato, dissolved yeast, eggs, sugar, butter, salt and orange zest. Split the vanilla pod lengthways and scrape out the seeds, then add them too. Using your hands, gradually mix all these ingredients together to form a smooth, elastic dough. Shape into a ball, wrap in clingfilm (plastic wrap) and leave to rest at room temperature for 30 minutes.

Remove the clingfilm and divide the dough into quarters. Roll each piece into a long sausage shape, about 15mm/⁵/₈ inch thick, and cut into 15cm/6 inch lengths. Form each length into a circle and seal the ends. Cover with a cloth and leave in a warm place for about 30 minutes, until they have doubled in size.

Heat the vegetable oil for deep frying in a large saucepan or deep-fryer until a small piece of bread dropped in sizzles immediately. Reduce the heat to medium and fry the doughnuts, a few at a time, turning, until golden on all sides. Drain on kitchen towel. Combine the sugar and cinnamon powder and coat the doughnuts. Serve warm or cold.

Contorni

On the side

We are lucky in Italy to have a wide variety of vegetables and salad ingredients. For this we must thank all the invaders who came to our country in ancient times, introducing us to delights such as olive trees, vines and citrus fruits, as well as a multitude of greens and even tomatoes. Generally we eat vegetables in season, and when I was young all the produce was local; some came from our garden, and anything bought from market stalls was picked that morning. Most of the herbs came from the hills above the village. Each season brought its specialities: with spring came tender sweet peas and broad (fava) beans, the first baby carrots, courgettes (zucchini), salad leaves, rocket (arugula), dandelion, spinach and asparagus and much more. As we went into summer, yellow, red, orange and green peppers of all shapes and sizes added colour and variety to the plate, as did aubergines (eggplant) and, of course, our beloved tomato. When the days became cooler and shorter and colourful leaves littered the ground, it was time to go foraging for wild mushrooms. Pumpkins took pride of place on market stalls, as did the first root vegetables: beetroot, carrots and potatoes. One of the few signs of life in winter was the pretty, purplish artichoke flowers growing in gardens, brightening up bleak days.

Vegetables played an important part in our diet and were eaten not only as a side dish, but also as a main course. Stuffing peppers, aubergines, onions and courgettes is a great way of making them go further and creating nutritious dishes for all the family. Vegetables are added to pasta and risotto and make bakes. The humble escarole, a lettuce-type vegetable, was often made into a main meal; I remember my nonna would fill it with all sorts of leftovers – bits of cheese, salami, stale bread, olives, capers – to make a nutritious meal for all the family.

Most Italians dress their vegetables and for a milder flavour good olive oil and lemon is all that is needed.

SERVES 4

salt and freshly ground black pepper

700g/1lb 9oz escarole, roughly chopped

4 tbsp extra virgin olive oil

1 large onion, finely chopped

4 thyme sprigs

200g/7oz frozen peas

200ml/7fl oz/scant 1 cup hot vegetable stock

1 garlic clove, left whole

50g/1³⁄₄oz pancetta or bacon, roughly chopped

Scarola e piselli

Escarole and peas

Escarole is popular in southern Italy and is the least bitter of the endive family. It resembles a large lettuce, but the outer leaves are coarser and quite tough, so it is always cooked. Escarole was common during the winter when I was a child, and we would have it often, either braised like this or filled with leftovers, as my nonna would make. I have combined the escarole with peas to make a healthy side dish to accompany meat. If you increase the quantities, it can be eaten on its own, with good bread, as a light meal.

Bring a medium saucepan of lightly salted water to the boil, add the escarole and cook for about 10 minutes, until tender. Drain well and set aside.

Meanwhile, heat 3 tbsp extra virgin olive oil in a large frying pan, add the onion and thyme and sweat on a medium heat for 5 minutes, or until softened. Add the peas, hot stock and a little pepper, cover with a lid and cook for a further 5 minutes.

Heat the remaining olive oil in another frying pan, add the garlic and pancetta and stir-fry on a medium–high heat for 5 minutes, or until golden. Add the escarole, some salt and pepper and cook for another 5 minutes. Reduce the heat to medium, add the pea mixture, mix well and cook for a further 5 minutes. Serve.

SERVES 4

250g/9oz asparagus, cleaned and
ends trimmed

salt

25g/1oz blanched almonds, toasted

12 fresh mint leaves

1 tbsp capers

4 tbsp extra virgin olive oil

Asparagi con pesto alle mandorle

Asparagus with almond pesto

In Italy I would always go out in spring to pick the long, thin wild asparagus. It was not until I came to England that I discovered the larger variety, which is ideal for dipping into sauces like this one. Almond pesto is common in Sicily for dressing pasta, and it marries really well with asparagus. This is an ideal starter or side dish, or to serve at parties.

Bring a medium saucepan of lightly salted water to the boil, add the asparagus and cook for about 5 minutes, until tender. Drain and arrange on a serving plate.

Blend the other ingredients to a fairly smooth consistency in a food processor and serve with the cooked asparagus.

Broccoli con aglio, olio e peperoncino

Sautéed long stem broccoli with garlic and chilli

SERVES 4

4 tbsp extra virgin olive oil

3 garlic cloves, thinly sliced

1 small red chilli (chile), finely chopped

400g/14oz long stem broccoli, stems trimmed

salt and freshly ground black pepper

juice of 1/2 lemon (optional)

Broccoli is such a nutritious vegetable and I especially like the long-stem or purple sprouting variety. I love it with lots of chilli (chile) and garlic, but for the children I add less chilli or omit it altogether. This makes a lovely accompaniment to sausages and other meat dishes, or can be enjoyed with bread as a light meal.

Heat the extra virgin olive oil in a frying pan, add the garlic and chilli and sweat for 1 minute on a medium–high heat. Add the broccoli and some salt and pepper and stir-fry for 1 minute. Add 150ml/5fl oz/²/₃ cup water, reduce the heat to medium, cover with a lid and cook for about 10 minutes, until tender.

Remove the lid, increase the heat and allow the liquid to evaporate. Remove from the heat, pour in the lemon juice, if using, and serve.

6 tbsp extra virgin olive oil

1 yellow (bell) pepper, deseeded and cut into strips

1 red (bell) pepper, deseeded and cut into strips

3 anchovy fillets in oil, drained (optional)

2 garlic cloves, thinly sliced

10 pitted green olives

1 tbsp capers

1 tbsp caster (superfine) sugar

4 tbsp white wine vinegar

salt and freshly ground black pepper

a small handful of curly parsley, roughly chopped

Peperoni all'agrodolce

Tangy peppers

This is a favourite recipe during the summer when (bell) peppers are abundant. Large batches were prepared in our house when I was a child and enjoyed cold throughout the day, for lunch, dinner or as a snack with bread. I make lots of it when the family comes round for a barbecue, or to have with cold roast meat. Once cooked, the longer you leave these peppers, the better the flavour. They are ideal for summer entertaining. Serve with lots of bread to mop up the juices.

Heat the extra virgin olive oil in a large frying pan, add all the pepper strips and cook on a medium-high heat until the skins are golden-brown. Add the anchovy fillets, if using, the garlic, olives and capers. Stir in the sugar, then add the vinegar and allow to evaporate. Reduce the heat to medium, cover with a lid and cook for about 5 minutes, or until the peppers are tender. Season to taste with salt and pepper and sprinkle over the parsley. Serve hot or cold, garnished with the parsley.

Insalata di pane bagnato

Bread salad

SERVES 4

3 tbsp red wine vinegar

4 slices of good country bread, about
1cm/$\frac{1}{2}$ inch thick

1 garlic clove, peeled

4 firm plum tomatoes, sliced

1 red onion, thinly sliced

1 small yellow (bell) pepper, deseeded and cut
into strips

85g/3oz cucumber, thinly sliced

2 celery stalks with leaves, thinly sliced

a handful of fresh basil leaves

6 tbsp extra virgin olive oil, plus extra to drizzle

salt and freshly ground black pepper

a pinch of dried oregano

This recipe has peasant origins. During the warmer season in areas of southern and central Italy, farmers would wet pieces of stale bread with home-made vinegar and eat them with whatever produce was available in the fields – tomatoes, cucumber, peppers. This makes a lovely, light meal and is very healthy. The vinegar really enhances the salad and makes you want to eat more. My daughter Olivia loves vinegar and raw crunchy vegetables, so why not try it out on your children for a healthy lunch? I'm sure they'll be impressed with all the wonderful colours of the salad and, of course, you can substitute other vegetables, depending on what you and your family prefer.

Dilute the vinegar with 4 tbsp water. Place a slice of bread on each serving plate. Rub the bread with garlic and drizzle with the vinegar mixture.

Place the sliced tomatoes, onion, pepper, cucumber, celery and basil leaves in a bowl, add the extra virgin olive oil, season with the salt, pepper and oregano and toss well.

Divide the salad between the slices of bread and leave to rest for about 10 minutes. Drizzle with extra virgin olive oil and serve.

Zucchini al cartoccio

Courgette chips with mint and vinegar

SERVES 4

2 tbsp red wine vinegar

1 garlic clove, peeled

500g/1lb 2oz courgettes (zucchini), cut into batons 4cm/1½ inch long

a handful of fresh mint leaves

plain (all-purpose) flour, to dust

good vegetable or seed oil, to deep-fry

salt

These Italian-type French fries are a great way to entice young children to eat green vegetables. This is a popular method of cooking courgettes (zucchini) in Italy. I have added mint and a drizzle of vinegar to enhance the flavour of the courgettes. It's a really tasty side dish, makes a great snack, or can even be served at children's parties. Try to serve the chips as soon as they are cooked or they will lose their crispiness.

Put the vinegar and garlic in a bowl, cover and leave to marinate for at least 2 hours.

Dust the courgette and mint in the flour, then shake off any excess. Heat the vegetable oil in a large saucepan or deep-fryer until a small piece of bread dropped in sizzles immediately. Fry the courgettes and mint until golden and crispy. Drain on kitchen towel. Sprinkle with salt and drizzle with the garlic-infused vinegar, then serve immediately.

Insalata di pinzimonio

Crunchy salad

- -

SERVES 4

2 fennel bulbs, trimmed and sliced
2 celery hearts, sliced
150g/5½oz radishes, sliced

for the dressing
4 tbsp extra virgin olive oil
3 tbsp lemon juice
salt and freshly ground black pepper

- -

Pinzimonio is the Italian equivalent of crudités, a selection of raw vegetables that are dipped in good extra virgin olive oil, salt and pepper and often served as antipasto or at parties. I remember in Italy the first spring vegetables were so fresh and flavoursome that all you needed was some extra virgin olive oil and a little salt. My father loved fennel and he would often eat raw chunks of it after a meal; he said it refreshed him and aided digestion. Fennel, celery and radishes are commonly included in this healthy, light vegetarian antipasto, which I have made into a crunchy salad with the addition of lemon juice in the dressing. If you prefer, you may omit the lemon juice and add more extra virgin olive oil. I also like lots of freshly ground black pepper. For maximum flavour, use very fresh vegetables, organic if possible.

Place the fennel, celery and radish in a large bowl. Whisk all the dressing ingredients together until the mixture thickens slightly, then pour over the salad and toss well.

8 tbsp extra virgin olive oil

2 large aubergines (eggplant),
cut into small cubes

4 red onions, finely chopped

2 tbsp capers

25 pitted (stoned) black olives,
cut into quarters

2 tbsp tomato purée (paste),
diluted in 6 tbsp water

1 tbsp caster (superfine) sugar

6 tbsp white wine vinegar

2 tbsp pine kernels

25g/1oz raisins, soaked in
lukewarm water and drained

salt and freshly ground black pepper

celery leaves, to garnish

Caponata

Sicilian sweet and sour aubergines

This traditional Sicilian dish is based on aubergines (eggplant), a popular vegetable on this southern Italian island. A lot of Sicilian dishes have Arab influences, and this accounts for the combination of the sweet and sour ingredients that really enhances the flavour of the aubergines and onions. This dish is often served cold as a starter, or as a side dish to accompany meat and fish. In the Naples area, an equivalent is known as *cianfotta*. I remember at the end of summer, when aubergines were abundant, we would often make a version of this and eat it cold with bread. To enjoy the dish at its best, make it the day before you plan to eat it and leave it in the fridge overnight for all the flavours to settle and infuse the aubergines.

Heat the extra virgin olive oil in a large frying pan and fry the aubergines on a medium-high heat until golden. Remove and drain on kitchen towel.

Reduce the heat to medium, then add the onions to the same pan and sweat until softened. Add the capers and olives and cook for 2 minutes. Stir in the diluted tomato purée and cook for about 5 minutes, until it begins to thicken slightly. Dilute the sugar in the vinegar and add to the pan along with the pine kernels, raisins and aubergines. Reduce the heat to low, half-cover with a lid and cook for 20 minutes. Season with salt and pepper to taste. Serve hot or cold, garnished with the celery leaves. If serving cold, refrigerate and remove 30 minutes before serving.

Carciofi alla Napoletana

Artichokes with olives and capers

4 globe artichokes
juice of 1 lemon
4 tbsp extra virgin olive oil
1 garlic clove, roughly chopped
a handful of fresh parsley, roughly chopped
25g/1oz pitted black olives, roughly chopped
1 tbsp capers, roughly chopped
75ml/2½fl oz/5 tbsp dry white wine
300ml/10fl oz/1¼ cups hot vegetable stock
freshly ground black pepper

Italians love the versatile globe artichoke, especially in the south, where it grows in abundance. They can be fried, roasted, filled, braised or eaten raw. I remember the artichoke vendors in my home village selling them roasted and the streets being filled with smoke; the smell was intoxicating and immediately made me hungry. This would always entice my father to buy some fresh from the market and cook them in a variety of ways. It was always his job to clean and cook them and my mother was never allowed to interfere. He would often braise them, as in this recipe, with olives and capers.

Clean the artichokes, removing the bottom outer leaves and trimming the tops. Cut off the stems and peel them, then slice lengthways and place in a bowl of water with the lemon juice (this will prevent discoloration). Cut the artichokes into quarters, discarding any hairs, and place them immediately in the lemon water.

Heat the extra virgin olive oil in a saucepan, add the garlic, parsley, olives and capers and sweat on a medium heat for 1 minute. Drain the artichokes, add to the pan and stir-fry for 3 minutes. Stir in the wine, then add the hot stock and some black pepper. Half-cover with a lid and cook on a medium heat for about 20 minutes. Remove the lid and continue to cook for 10 minutes, until the artichokes are cooked through and the liquid has reduced by at least half.

SERVES 4

1kg/2lb 4oz new baby potatoes

salt and freshly ground black pepper

4 tbsp extra virgin olive oil

1 garlic clove, thinly sliced

2 bay leaves

a pinch of dried oregano

leaves from 1 fresh rosemary sprig

leaves from 1 fresh thyme sprig

Le patate arrosto di Adriana

Adriana's roast potatoes

I love these roast potatoes. My sister Adriana makes them whenever she roasts meat. The herbs really bring out the taste of the new potatoes. They're easy to prepare and quick to cook.

Preheat the oven to 220°C/425°F/gas mark 7.

Wash and scrub the potatoes, but do not peel them. Place in a saucepan of lightly salted water, bring to the boil and cook for 5 minutes. Remove from the heat and drain. Place in a roasting pan together with the rest of the ingredients and, using your hands, toss well. Cover with foil and roast for 10 minutes, then remove the foil and roast for a further 15 minutes, until golden and cooked through.

Insalata di bietole rosse con cipollotti

Beetroot and spring onion salad

SERVES 4–6

700g/1lb 9oz beetroot

a small bunch of spring onions (scallions), shredded

for the dressing
8 tbsp extra virgin olive oil

3 tbsp red wine vinegar

2 garlic cloves, thinly sliced

a handful of chives, finely chopped

salt and freshly ground black pepper, to taste

Although more commonly associated with Eastern Europe than Italy, beetroot was a favourite of my mother's. Perhaps it was her Russian ancestry that made her love it. She would often have it simply dressed with some extra virgin olive oil or, when she had a glut, she would boil it in vinegar and preserve it in lots of olive oil. It is also one of my wife Liz's favourite vegetables, and she loves it in a simple salad with spring onions (scallions). My daughters, too, have taken a liking to beetroot and we look forward to the end of summer when my friend Paolo brings wonderful organic beetroot in all shapes, sizes and colours from his allotment.

Wash and scrub the beetroot under cold running water. Place it in a saucepan with plenty of cold water and bring to the boil, then reduce the heat to low and simmer for about $1^1/_2$ hours, until the beetroot is tender.

Meanwhile, combine all the dressing ingredients together in a small bowl.

Drain the beetroot and pat dry with a clean cloth. Remove the skins with the help of the cloth. Cut the flesh into quarters or slices, depending on the size of the beetroot, and place in a serving bowl with the spring onions. Pour the dressing over and leave for 20 minutes. Discard the garlic slices before serving if you wish.

PANE

Dough

There is an old Italian saying, 'Buono come il pane' (literally 'as good as bread'), when talking about a good person because that is exactly what bread is. For me, bread is everything. When you have it, you need little else. It is healthy, nutritious and feeds the soul. In Italy it is served at each meal and bought fresh each day from the panetteria (bakery).

The smell of freshly baked bread evokes warm feelings of home and family. My mother used to make it every Thursday. It was a ritual; she would light the wood-fired oven the night before and wake up extra early the next morning to stoke the fire. As the loaves baked, the smell would slowly waft through the house and immediately had me out of bed and into the kitchen. A few cooked loaves would be on the kitchen table, others still in the oven. She would often add sugar and perhaps some dried fruit and citrus zest to the remaining dough to make a pane dolce (sweet bread, see page 195). I loved to tear the first loaf apart and eat the warm bread – the taste was heavenly.

Long after we had all left the family home, my mother would make bread when we went to visit. In those early days, when I travelled to and from Italy by train, she would often enrich it with ham, salami and cheese, and give it to me for the journey back. Being a young man, I didn't really want to have a knapsack, but she always insisted and I was so glad, because on that long, melancholic journey through France during the night, when I felt lonely and hungry, the taste of my mother's bread and the memories of home it evoked soon filled me with warmth and happiness.

Bread means tradition. It is made all over the world, in different ways, but the basic ingredients are the same. In Italy it is never thrown away – that would be a sin, and old wives' tales said that if you did, bad luck would be bestowed upon you. Bread was thought to be holy food and a gift from God. Leftover, stale bread was always used up, for breadcrumbs, in panzanella (bread salad), as fillings, or put back in the oven to double-bake as a hard biscuit-type bread.

I love to bake bread. In fact, I should have been a baker. A few years ago I had a wood-fired oven built in my garden and have tried to recreate the look and atmosphere of the one we had at home when I was a child. When I get lost in nostalgia for my childhood, this little corner of the garden fills me with warm feelings. When I plan to bake, I get up very early in the morning to light the oven, and I love to hear the crackling of the fire almost speaking to me. I prepare the flour, yeast, salt and water and always make sure I talk to the dough before leaving it to rise. If I talk nicely to it, it will rise well and produce excellent bread!

In Italy we make a variety of savoury breads, such as the pane pasquale, a round loaf filled with cheese and salami and topped with boiled eggs to represent Easter. When I was a child, savoury breads were common in rural areas as a quick and easy lunch for farmers whilst working in the fields. These are still made today to be enjoyed on picnics and journeys, just like my mother used to do for me. And the famous Italian Christmas cake, panettone, is made from dough.

I like to make pizza when friends come round. I usually make tons of dough – Liz always tells me off for making too much, but I just can't help it. I get everyone involved and ask all my guests to top their own pizza and bake it in the very hot oven. I love to see their amazed expressions when, after a few minutes, a delicious hot pizza emerges. It's great being outside because you can make a real mess and it doesn't matter. I shape any remaining dough into loaves and bake these towards the end of the day, so all my guests can take some home. There are usually lots more left, so I send the girls off with loaves for the neighbours (but of course, not before they have had a slice of freshly baked warm bread smeared with lots of butter). The next day for breakfast, they always ask for 'Toast with Daddy's bread!' I love to see them just as excited as I was when my mother used to bake bread.

12g/$\frac{1}{4}$oz fresh yeast

325ml/11fl oz/scant 1$\frac{1}{2}$ cups
lukewarm water

500g/1lb 2oz/3$\frac{1}{2}$ cups Italian '00' flour
or strong plain (all-purpose bread) flour,
plus extra to dust

2 tsp salt

Impasto per pane
Bread dough

So simple and yet so nutritious and wholesome. There is nothing more satisfying to me than making my own bread. This recipe is for a plain loaf, or it can be formed into rolls. It is one of the nicest things you can make for your family. It will keep for about a week, or even longer, and is great sliced and made into bruschetta or toasted for breakfast.

Dissolve the yeast in the water. Combine the flour and salt on a clean work surface or in a large bowl, make a well in the centre, then gradually pour in the dissolved yeast liquid and mix to form a soft but not sticky dough – if necessary, add a little more lukewarm water. Lightly flour a clean work surface and knead the dough well for about 5 minutes, until smooth and elastic. Place on a clean tea towel,

brush the top with water to prevent it from drying out, then cover with another clean, slightly damp tea towel. Leave to rise in a warm place for about 30 minutes, or until the dough has doubled in size.

Shape the dough into a loaf and put in a 450g/1lb loaf tin (pan), or on a flat baking sheet. Cover and leave to rise in a warm place for 30 minutes. Preheat the oven to 250°C/480°F/gas mark 9.

Place the loaf in the oven, reduce the temperature to 240°C/475°F/gas mark 8 and bake for about 20 minutes, until golden. To test if the loaf is ready, remove from the loaf tin (if using) and gently tap it on the bottom – if it sounds hollow, it is ready. Leave to cool on a wire rack. It is very tempting to slice it as soon as you can handle it and spread it with butter!

La pizza di Olivia

Olivia's pizza

Olivia's favourite food is pizza, but she really enjoys sausages and broccoli too, so we combined them together. (Sausages with broccoli is actually a very common dish in southern Italy; the broccoli used is the *cime di rapa* (rape tops), slightly bitter-tasting with lots of leaves, which are also cooked.) This pizza is highly nutritious and filling, and really a meal on its own.

Make the pizza dough as described on page 183.

Preheat the oven to its highest setting.

Heat the extra virgin olive oil in a large frying pan, add the garlic and chilli, if using, and sweat on a medium–high heat for a couple of minutes. Add the broccoli, sausage and salt to taste and sauté for 1 minute. Cover with a lid, reduce the heat to medium and cook for 15 minutes.

Meanwhile, prepare the bases. Sprinkle a little flour on a clean work surface and, using your fingers, spread a piece of dough into a circle roughly 28–30cm/11–12 inches in diameter. The dough must be very thin, but be careful not to tear it. Repeat with the other ball of dough. Sprinkle some breadcrumbs, flour or semolina over 2 large flat baking sheets and place the pizza bases on them.

Remove the sausage and broccoli from the heat. Put the tomatoes in a bowl, season with salt and pepper and a drizzle of extra virgin olive oil, and stir. Spoon the tomatoes over the pizza bases, then scatter with the sausages and broccoli and drizzle with extra virgin olive oil. Reduce the oven to 220°C/425°F/gas mark 7 and bake the pizzas for about 8 minutes, or until cooked.

La pizza di Chloe

Chloe's pizza

MAKES 2 LARGE PIZZAS

10g/^{1}/$_4$oz fresh yeast or 1 x 7g sachet of dried

325ml/11fl oz/scant 1^1/$_2$ cups lukewarm water

500g/1lb 2oz/3^1/$_2$ cups strong plain (all-purpose bread) flour, plus extra to dust

2 tsp salt

dried breadcrumbs, flour or semolina, to dust

400g can chopped plum tomatoes, optional

for the topping

extra virgin olive oil, to drizzle

2 balls of mozzarella, roughly chopped

6 slices of Parma ham, roughly torn

The topping on this pizza includes Chloe's favourite ingredients. This type of *pizza bianca* is not traditional, but has become popular in *pizzerie* all over Italy during the last 20 years.

Dissolve the fresh yeast in the water (if you are using easy-blend/active dry yeast, just mix it in with the flour). Combine the flour and salt for the dough in a large bowl, then gradually add the dissolved yeast liquid (or dried yeast and water), mixing well to form a dough. Shape the dough into a ball, cover with a cloth and leave to rest for 5 minutes.

Knead the dough for 10 minutes, until smooth and elastic, then split in half. Knead each piece for 2 minutes, then shape into a ball. Sprinkle some flour on a clean tea towel or baking sheet and place the dough on it. Cover with a slightly damp cloth and leave to rise in a warm place for at least 1 hour.

Preheat the oven to its highest setting.

Sprinkle a little flour on a clean work surface and, using your fingers, spread a piece of dough into a circle roughly 28–30cm/11–12 inches in diameter. The dough must be very thin, but be careful not to tear it. Repeat with the other ball of dough. Sprinkle some breadcrumbs, flour or semolina over 2 large flat baking sheets and place the pizza bases on them.

If using the tomatoes, put them in a bowl, season with salt and pepper and a drizzle of extra virgin olive oil, and stir. Spoon the tomatoes over the pizza bases (if not using tomatoes, just drizzle the bases with extra virgin olive oil). Arrange the mozzarella pieces on top, followed by the Parma ham. Reduce the oven temperature to 220°C/425°F/gas mark 7 and bake the pizzas for about 8 minutes, or until cooked. Remove from the oven, top with the rocket and drizzle with some more extra virgin olive oil.

**MAKES 1 X 28CM/11-INCH
ROUND SFINCIONE**

1 quantity of basic bread dough (see page 177)

6 tbsp extra virgin olive oil, plus extra to grease

1 large red onion, thinly sliced

500g/1lb 2oz canned cherry tomatoes

salt and freshly ground black pepper

25g/1oz anchovies in oil, drained

60g/2¼oz caciocavallo cheese,

Sfincione Siciliano

Sicilian focaccia

The *sfincione* is a traditional focaccia from Palermo in Sicily, and was originally baked by the nuns at the San Vito monastery and served at Christmas as a richer variety of bread. In modern Palermo it is found in *rosticcerie*, and sold by street vendors from their three-wheeler vehicles. The word *'sfincione'* derives from *'sfincia'*, meaning 'something very soft', which indeed the dough is. Normally, sardines are added to the rich tomato topping, but I have substituted anchovies instead. Caciocavallo cheese is a typical southern Italian cheese that can be found in good delis; however, you can use provolone or Parmesan instead. This is a delicious snack, perfect for the whole family to share.

Make the bread dough as described on page 177.

While the bread is rising, make the sauce. Heat 2 tbsp extra virgin olive oil in a saucepan, add the onion and sweat on a medium heat until softened. Add the tomatoes and season with salt and pepper, then cover with a lid, reduce the heat to low and

cook for 20 minutes. Five minutes before the end of cooking time add the anchovies. Preheat the oven to 220°C/425°F/gas mark 7.

When the bread dough has risen, add the remaining extra virgin olive oil to it and, using your hands, knead it in well. Initially you may feel that the oil is not being absorbed, but continue to knead for about 10 minutes and it will be evenly distributed.

Gently grease a 28cm/11 inch round baking sheet with olive oil and place the dough on it. Using your fingers, spread it around to the edges. Scatter the cheese all over the dough and top with the tomato and anchovy sauce.

Reduce the oven temperature to 200°C/400°F/gas mark 6 and bake the sfincione for 35 minutes. Transfer to a wire rack and leave to cool.

Ciambella all'acciughe e olive

Anchovy and olive bread

SERVES 4

4 tbsp extra virgin olive oil, plus extra to grease

85g/3oz anchovies in oil, drained

50g/1³/₄oz/4 tbsp butter

500g/1lb 2oz/3¹/₂ cups '00' flour or strong plain
(all-purpose bread) flour, plus extra to dust

1 x 7g sachet of dried yeast

4 eggs

85g/3oz mixed green and black olives, pitted
and finely chopped

Ciambella usually means a sweet ring cake, but nowadays it refers to savoury cakes too. This recipe uses bread dough enriched with eggs, with the addition of olives and anchovies. It can be eaten on its own, with cured meats and cheese, or as an accompaniment to main meals.

Heat 2 tbsp extra virgin olive oil in a small frying pan. Add the anchovies (keeping 2 aside for later) and cook on a low heat until they dissolve. Remove from the heat and stir in the butter until melted.

Combine the flour, yeast and eggs in a large bowl. Add the anchovy mixture and olives and mix well to form a smooth dough. Knead on a lightly floured surface for 10 minutes, then cover with a clean tea towel and leave in a warm place for 1¹/₂ hours.

Preheat the oven to 220°C/425°F/gas mark 7. Grease a 20cm/8-inch ring cake pan with extra virgin olive oil and line with greaseproof paper, then grease the paper with oil.

Knead the dough for a minute, then shape it to fit the tin. Finely slice lengthways the remaining 2 anchovy fillets. Using a sharp knife, make incisions on top of the bread and insert a sliver of anchovy into each cut. Bake for 40 minutes, then leave to rest for 5 minutes. Slice and serve.

Calzoncini

Small calzoni filled with cheese

- -

MAKES 10 CALZONCINI

1 x 7g sachet of dried yeast

75ml/2¹/₂fl oz/5 tbsp lukewarm water

250g/9oz/1²/₃ cups '00' flour or strong plain (all-purpose bread) flour, plus extra to dust

1 egg

2 tsp extra virgin olive oil

good vegetable or seed oil to deep-fry

for the filling

1 tbsp extra virgin olive oil

a knob of butter

1 red onion, thinly sliced

100g/3¹/₂oz ricotta

100g/3¹/₂oz mozzarella, cut into small cubes

20g/³/₄oz Parmesan, grated

a handful of fresh basil leaves, finely chopped

salt and freshly ground black pepper

- -

Calzoncini are a type of filled pizza that are deep-fried. Popular throughout southern Italy, they were a treat my father would buy from the local rosticcieria when I was out with him. They were also made at home with leftover bread dough and especially liked by children, who would wait by the stove as the calzoncini were lifted out of the oil. They make a lovely nutritious snack and are ideal for children's parties. I have used a traditional filling of red onion and three cheeses, but you could use tomato or ham.

First, make the dough. Dissolve the yeast in the water. Place the flour in a large bowl or on a clean work surface. Make a well in the centre and gradually add the yeasted water, egg and extra virgin olive oil, mixing well to form a smooth dough.

Knead on a lightly floured surface for 10 minutes. Take pieces of dough, each weighing about 40g/1¹/₂oz, and form into balls, then flatten slightly and place on a tray. Cover with a clean tea towel and leave to rise in a warm place for 1 hour.

For the filling, heat the extra virgin olive oil and butter in a small frying pan, add the onion, cover the pan with a lid and cook on a low heat for about 10 minutes, or until the onion has softened. Remove from the heat and leave to cool.

Combine the ricotta, mozzarella, Parmesan, basil, salt, pepper and cooled onion in a bowl and set aside.

Take each piece of dough and roll out on a lightly floured surface into a circle about 10cm/4 inches in diameter and about 3mm/¹/₈ inch thick. Place a spoonful of filling in the centre of each, brush water around the edges and fold the dough over, sealing well – make sure the filling does not escape.

Heat vegetable oil for deep frying in a pan or deep-fryer. When hot, fry the calzoncini in batches until golden. Drain on kitchen towel and serve hot or cold.

Sformato di pane alle verdure

Italian vegetable pie

- - - - - - - - - - - - - - - - - -

SERVES 6–8

1 x 7g sachet of dried yeast

150ml/5fl oz/²/₃ cup lukewarm water

250g/9oz/1²/₃ cups '00' flour or strong plain
(all-purpose bread) flour, plus extra to dust

25g/1oz/2 tbsp softened butter, cut
into pieces

for the filling

3 tbsp extra virgin olive oil, plus extra to brush
and drizzle

500g/1lb 2oz potatoes

salt and freshly ground black pepper

1 small onion, thinly sliced

300g/10¹/₂oz courgettes (zucchini), thinly sliced

4 artichokes preserved in oil, sliced
(reserve 2 tbsp of the oil)

600g/1lb 5oz spinach

2 eggs

50g/1³/₄oz Parmesan, grated

- - - - - - - - - - - - - - - - - -

Pies are not normally associated with Italian cooking, but in Campania it is traditional to make a savoury pie during Christmas. It is made with leftover bread dough enriched with lard and escarole, mixed with anchovies, capers, pine kernels and olives. The pie is a nutritious snack, which farmers used to take with them to the fields for lunch, and I remember finding a slice in my school lunchbox – a treat my nonna (grandmother) would put in, as she made the pie for my nonno (grandfather), who loved it. I have made a lighter version – and believe me, once you start on a slice, you will want more.

Dissolve the yeast in the water. Combine the flour, butter and a pinch of salt in a large bowl. Make a well in the centre, gradually pour in the yeasted water and mix well to form a soft but not sticky dough. Knead on a lightly floured surface for 10 minutes, then form into a ball, cover with a clean tea towel and leave to rise in a warm place for 2 hours.

Preheat the oven to 200°C/400°F/gas mark 6. Lightly grease a baking sheet with olive oil.

Peel the potatoes and slice into rounds about 5mm/¹/₄ inch thick. Place on the baking sheet, sprinkle with salt and pepper and drizzle with extra virgin olive oil. Roast for about 15 minutes, until cooked through but firm.

Meanwhile, heat 3 tbsp extra virgin olive oil in a frying pan, add the onion, then sweat over a medium heat until it has softened. Add the courgettes and sauté on a medium heat for 10 minutes until softened. Add the artichokes with their oil and cook for 5 minutes. Add the spinach and salt and pepper to taste, cover with a lid and cook for 5 minutes. Allow to cool.

Increase the oven temperature to 220°C/425°F/gas mark 7. Beat the eggs in a bowl, then stir in the Parmesan and some salt and pepper. Add the cooled vegetables and gently combine.

Line a round 23cm/9 inch diameter pie dish with greaseproof paper. Divide the dough in half. Roll out one half on a lightly floured surface and line the bottom and sides of the pie dish. Arrange the cooked potatoes on the bottom, followed by the vegetable filling. Roll out the other piece of dough and cover the pie, sealing well so that the filling does not escape. Prick all over with a fork and brush with extra virgin olive oil. Bake in the oven for 30–35 minutes, until golden. Can be eaten hot or cold.

Panini al Parmigiano

Parmesan bread rolls

MAKES 16 ROLLS

500g/1lb 2oz/3½ cups '0' flour or strong plain (all-purpose bread) flour, plus extra to dust

85g/3oz Parmesan, grated

1 x 7g sachet of dried yeast

2 tsp salt

40ml/1½fl oz/scant 3 tbsp extra virgin olive oil

250ml/9fl oz/generous 1 cup lukewarm water

This recipe came about by mistake – I was once making some bread rolls and instead of salt I grabbed Parmesan. Although annoyed with myself at first, I decided to add more cheese and see what the result would be. Well, they were a success, as you can see by the inclusion of this recipe in the book. The Parmesan gives a really nice taste, as well as making them more nutritious. They're fun to make with the children, who, of course, can make any shape they like.

Put all the dry ingredients into a large bowl or on a clean work surface. Make a well in the centre and add the extra virgin olive oil, then gradually add the water and mix to a smooth dough. Knead for 10 minutes, then cover with a clean tea towel and leave to rise for 1½ hours.

Knead the dough for 1 minute, then divide into small pieces, each weighing about 40g/1½oz. Roll out each piece on a lightly floured surface into a thin sausage about 22cm/8½ inch in length and wrap round into a coil. Using kitchen scissors, snip around the edge for a decorative effect, if desired. Cover and leave to rise for a further 40 minutes.

Preheat the oven to 220°C/425°F/gas mark 7. Lightly flour a non-stick baking sheet.

Place the rolls on the baking sheet and bake for 15–20 minutes, until golden. Cool on a wire rack.

Pane dolce

Sweet bread cake

- - - - - - - - - - - - - - - - - - -

MAKES 1 X 20CM/8-INCH ROUND CAKE

2 egg yolks

70g/2^1/$_2$oz/^{1}/$_3$ cup caster (superfine) sugar

50g/1^3/$_4$oz/scant 4 tbsp softened butter, cut into
pieces, plus extra to grease

40g/1^1/$_2$oz mixed candied peel

finely grated zest of 1 orange

a pinch of ground cinnamon

a pinch of salt

about 100g/3^1/$_2$oz/^{2}/$_3$ cup '00' flour or strong
plain (all-purpose bread) flour, plus extra to dust

icing sugar, to dust

for the dough

1 x 7g sachet of dried yeast

100ml/3^1/$_2$fl oz/^{1}/$_3$ cup lukewarm water

250g/9oz/1^2/$_3$ cups '00' flour or strong plain
(all-purpose bread) flour

- - - - - - - - - - - - - - - - - - -

Making sweet bread-type cakes is very popular in
Italy. It originated as *cucina povera* when people
wanted something sweet but could not afford it.
My mother and grandmother normally made it
with leftover bread dough and added a little sugar,
eggs and whatever else was available – dried fruit,
lemon or orange zest. It is made all over Italy and
known by different names, such as *stiacciata* in
Tuscany, or even *focaccia*, as we often called it. The
sweetened bread dough was baked and eaten at
teatime or at breakfast, dipped into warm milk. It is
delicious served toasted with jam and makes an
ideal snack for hungry children after school.

For the dough, dissolve the yeast in the water. Place
the flour in a large bowl or on a clean work surface.
Make a well in the centre and gradually add the
yeasted water, mixing well to form a smooth dough.
Knead on a lightly floured work surface for
10 minutes. Form into a ball, cover with a clean tea
towel and leave to rest in a warm place for 1 hour.

Meanwhile, whisk the egg yolks, sugar and butter
until creamy. Stir in the candied peel, orange zest,
cinnamon and salt. Place the risen dough on a work
surface, then flatten with your hands and gradually
work the egg mixture into the dough, adding a little
flour as you do. You will find this is a sticky operation,
but just keep adding the flour gradually and it will
become a soft dough.

Lightly grease and flour a 20cm/8-inch round cake
tin. Place the dough in the tin, cover with a clean tea
towel and leave to rise in a warm place for 1 hour.

Preheat the oven to 190°C/375°F/gas mark 5.

When the dough has risen, bake for 30 minutes, or
until golden. Leave to cool in the tin.

To serve, turn out of the tin, dust with icing sugar and
slice crossways, as you would bread.

Dolci

Sweet

When I was a child, dessert was usually fresh fruit. As soon as the main course was over, my mother would put the fruit bowl on the table so we could help ourselves. I loved picking cherries, peaches, apricots, wild strawberries and, my favourite at the end of summer, figs. I always knew where the best fruit was and which tree had the ripest – I checked daily. When I brought home lots of fruit, my mother would transform it into jams, cakes and crostate (tarts), which I would enjoy for merenda (afternoon snack). If I picked morello cherries she would put them in jars with sugar and leave them in the sun for a few days, until the sugar had dissolved and a wonderful cherry syrup was left, which would be used in ice cream and pasticiotto (a type of cherry pie).

Most desserts, cakes and biscuits were made at home by women. My grandmother's speciality was apple cake, my mother's was fruit tart and my sisters would experiment with biscuits, fruit salads and ice cream. Sweet treats were usually made from leftovers – bread dough was used to make pan dolce or sweet pies and a glut of fruit would go into tarts and cakes. We also enjoyed ricotta as a dessert; this was freshly made and sometimes served warm with a little sugar or cinnamon sprinkled over the top. A lot of southern Italian cakes and pastries include ricotta – for instance the Sicilian cassata (see page 214) and cannoli (little filled tubes of pastry dough), as well as tarts and cakes.

There was a small pasticcieria in our village of Minori, and sometimes, usually for a special occasion, we would buy cakes there. We knew the family who owned it and now and then I helped with odd jobs such as skinning almonds (not the most glamorous of tasks); it was interesting to watch the pasticciere (pastry chef) at work. The pasticcieria has grown considerably since I left and is now quite a famous spot to enjoy their lemon cakes. I love desserts and have a very sweet tooth; I don't have much time to make them these days, but when I do I tend to recreate my mother's fruit crostate (see page 210).

Gelatina di vino bianco con frutti di bosco

White wine jelly with fruits of the forest and strawberry sauce

SERVES 4

1 leaf or sheet of gelatine

200ml/7fl oz/scant 1 cup dry white wine

70g/2¹/₂oz/¹/₃ cup caster (superfine) sugar

¹/₂ clove

1cm/¹/₂ inch piece of cinnamon stick

25g/1oz raspberries

25g/1oz blueberries

4 fresh mint leaves, plus extra to decorate

4 tsp good natural yogurt

for the strawberry sauce

100g/3¹/₂oz strawberries, hulled, plus extra, sliced, to decorate

juice of ¹/₂ lemon

2 tbsp caster (superfine) sugar

Jelly (jello) in desserts is not traditionally Italian, but it has become popular in restaurants and at home, particularly for children's parties. I like this recipe for summer entertaining, to make use of the season's berries. It looks stunning served in small liqueur glasses. Because of the alcohol content, the portions are small. For children, substitute freshly squeezed orange or elderflower juice for the wine.

Place the gelatine in a bowl of cold water to soften. Meanwhile, combine the wine, sugar, clove and cinnamon stick in a small saucepan and place over a medium heat. Bring to the boil, then boil rapidly for 3 minutes, until the sugar has dissolved. Remove from the heat and remove and discard the clove and cinnamon. Drain the gelatine, squeeze out the excess water, then stir the gelatine into the liquid and leave to cool.

Meanwhile, blend all the ingredients for the sauce to a smooth consistency in a food processor, then cover and refrigerate.

Divide the cooled jelly liquid between 4 x 100ml/3¹/₂fl oz liqueur glasses, filling them to just over halfway. Drop a few raspberries, blueberries and a mint leaf in each glass. Place in the fridge for 6 hours, or until the jelly has set. When set, top the jellies with the strawberry sauce, then a dollop of yogurt, and decorate with strawberry slices and mint leaves. Cover and store in the fridge until required.

2 peaches, pitted

2 white peaches, pitted

4 apricots, pitted

4 kiwi fruit, peeled

200g/7oz strawberries, hulled

100g/3^1/$_2$oz blueberries

100g/3^1/$_2$oz/^{1}/$_2$ cup caster
(superfine) sugar

juice of ^{1}/$_2$ lemon

juice of 1 large orange

a few fresh mint leaves, to decorate

Macedonia estiva

Summer fruit salad

For me, fruit is the best dessert, and what better way to celebrate summer than by putting all the season's fruits together. *Macedonia* (fruit salad) has always been popular in Italy. Different fruits are used depending on the season, but sugar and citrus fruits are typically used for the dressing. Once the fruit has been left to macerate, a lovely sweet syrup develops and enhances the taste of the fruit. This simple summer dessert is delicious served with lemon sorbet (sherbet), if desired, and can be enjoyed by all the family or when entertaining. Easy, nutritious and packed with vitamins, it makes a refreshing end to a meal.

Slice the peaches, white peaches, apricots, kiwi fruit and strawberries and place in a large bowl with the blueberries.

Combine the sugar with the lemon and orange juices in a small bowl and mix well until the sugar has dissolved. Pour over the fruit, decorate with mint leaves, cover and allow to macerate for at least 30 minutes before serving.

Il gelato della nonna Fausta

Nonna Fausta's ice cream

SERVES 4

2 egg yolks

250g/9oz/1¼ cups caster (superfine) sugar

500ml/18fl oz/generous 2 cups milk

6cm/2½ inch vanilla pod (bean), split

6 slices of unwaxed lemon peel

biscuits such as savoiardi, to serve

This recipe comes from my wife Liz's grandmother, who used to make it for her during the annual summer visit to Italy. Two aluminium trays of it were always in the freezer: one vanilla and one chocolate. This is the traditional way of making ice cream and, according to Nonna Fausta, the secret is getting the sugar content right. When I recreated this recipe, it took me back to my childhood days and my immediate reaction was 'sapore genuino' ('it has the genuine taste!').

Beat together the egg yolks and sugar until creamy. Add the milk and whisk well. Add the vanilla pod and lemon peel. Pour into a saucepan, place over a gentle heat, stirring well all the time, until almost boiling. Remove from the heat and leave to cool, then remove the vanilla pod and lemon peel.

Place in a plastic container and freeze for 6 hours, removing from the freezer every 20 minutes to stir gently but thoroughly. Continue to do this for about 6 hours. (Alternatively, once your cream has cooled, place in the ice-cream maker and follow the instructions, then put in the freezer.)

Serve the ice cream in scoops in glasses with savoiardi biscuits.

For chocolate ice cream

To make a chocolate ice cream, make as above, but omit the vanilla and lemon peel. When you remove the pan from the heat, gradually add 25g/1oz good sifted unsweetened cocoa powder, whisking well to avoid lumps. Then proceed with the freezing process by hand or machine.

MAKES ABOUT 10 LOLLIES

150g/5¹/₂oz strawberries, hulled

3 egg yolks

75g/2³/₄oz/¹/₃ cup caster
(superfine) sugar

a pinch of salt

150ml/5fl oz/²/₃ cup milk

100ml/3¹/₂fl oz/¹/₃ cup double
(heavy) cream

6 fresh mint leaves

finely grated zest of 1 large
unwaxed lemon

- - - - - - - - - - - - - - - - - - - -

Ghiaccioli al limone e fragole

Lemon and strawberry ice pops

The consistency of these ice pops is more like ice cream, while the combination of lemon, strawberries and a slight mint infusion works really well. Placing thin slices of strawberry on the sides of the moulds (molds) gives a pretty effect when the lollies are unmoulded. Make sure you get good moulds, as it can be tricky to remove the lollies when set. (If you prefer, you can make the mixture in a container and serve as ice cream instead.) The children will enjoy making these with you.

Slice half the strawberries very finely and arrange on the sides of 10 x 80ml ice pop moulds (molds). Immediately freeze for 30 minutes. Finely chop the remaining strawberries and set aside.

Using an electric whisk, whisk the egg yolks, sugar and salt together in a bowl until creamy and the sugar has dissolved.

Place the milk, cream and mint leaves in a saucepan and gently heat (do not boil). Remove from the heat and leave to cool slightly, then stir in the egg mixture. Return to a low heat and cook for about 1 minute, stirring all the time, until slightly thickened. Remove from the heat and stir in the chopped strawberries and lemon zest. Pour into the moulds and freeze for at least 6 hours.

Semifreddo di zabaglione con salsa di fragole

Zabaglione semifreddo with strawberry sauce

- - - - - - - - - - - - - - - - - - - -

SERVES 4

4 egg yolks

60g/2¹/₄oz/generous ¹/₄ cup caster (superfine) sugar

150ml/5fl oz/²/₃ cup Marsala

200ml/7fl oz/scant 1 cup double (heavy) cream

for the strawberry sauce

150g/5¹/₂oz strawberries, hulled

25g/1oz/2 tbsp caster (superfine) sugar

1 tbsp lemon juice

- - - - - - - - - - - - - - - - - - - -

A type of zabaglione was made for me most mornings when I was in a hurry and would not sit down to breakfast. My mother would whisk up an egg, some sugar and a little hot milk in a cup. Often, if I left the house without it, she would come after me with cup in hand and I would have to drink it all up, sometimes in front of my friends, which embarrassed me. However, as a treat, I remember her telling me she would add a drop of Marsala. She insisted this was a quick but highly nutritious breakfast, which would give me lots of energy. With these few simple ingredients, I came up with a delicious semifreddo. It can be made in one container or, if you want to impress guests for a dinner party, individual ones made in paper cups or dariole moulds look lovely too.

For the sauce, blend all the ingredients to a smooth consistency in a food processor, then cover and place in the fridge.

For the zabaglione, whisk together the egg yolks and sugar in a heatproof bowl, then place over a saucepan of gently simmering water and whisk for 5 minutes. Gradually add the Marsala, whisking well, until the mixture has doubled in size. Remove from the heat and leave to cool. Whisk the double cream until stiff, then fold into the egg mixture.

Line a rectangular plastic or silicone 15 x 10cm/ 6 x 4-inch mould (mold) with clingfilm (plastic wrap) and pour in the zabaglione. Freeze for 3 hours.

When required, remove from the freezer and leave to stand for a minute, then tip out on a plate, divide into 4 portions and serve with the strawberry sauce.

MAKES ABOUT 18

2 egg whites

115g/4oz/generous ½ cup caster
(superfine) sugar

2 tbsp strong espresso coffee

Meringhe al caffè
Coffee meringues

My wife Liz's grandmother often made meringues for the grandchildren at teatime. To give the meringues a twist, I have added coffee, and these go really well with a cup of freshly made steaming espresso, ideally served after a meal. If you don't like coffee, especially if making this for children, substitute water for the espresso (although my daughter Olivia loves these). You can make more by increasing the quantities; the meringues can be stored in an airtight container for about a month. They are great for coeliacs.

Preheat the oven to 120°C/250°F/gas mark ½.

Line a baking sheet with non-stick greaseproof paper. Whisk the egg whites in a clean glass bowl until stiff peaks form.

Put the sugar and espresso coffee in a small saucepan and cook on a low heat, stirring all the time, until it boils, then boil and stir for 2 minutes. Remove from the heat and gradually add to the stiffened egg whites, whisking until it is well amalgamated.

Place spoonfuls of the meringue on the prepared baking sheet and bake for 2 hours, or until the meringues have dried out and look smooth and shiny. Cool on a wire rack, then store in an airtight container.

175g/6oz/1¼ cups plain (all-purpose)
flour, plus extra to dust

75g/2¾oz/6 tbsp cold butter, plus extra
to grease

75g/2¾oz/⅓ cup caster (superfine)
sugar

finely grated zest of 1 unwaxed lemon

2 egg yolks

1 x 250ml/9fl oz/generous 1 cup
of strawberry jam (see page 232)

1 egg, beaten

icing (confectioner's) sugar, sifted,
to dust

Crostata di Mamma

My mum's jam tart

Simple homemade jam or fruit tarts like this one are common all over Italy, made by mammas for their children, usually for *merenda* (teatime). My mum used to make this tart for us, filled with her delicious strawberry jam. The pastry is simple to make and, if you make a large quantity, it can be frozen to use later. By preparing your own pastry and filling, you can create a simple and nutritious sweet treat.

To make the pastry, put the flour on a clean work surface and rub in the butter until the mixture resembles breadcrumbs. Add the sugar, lemon zest and egg yolks and mix well to form a smooth dough. Shape into a ball, wrap in clingfilm (plastic wrap) and leave in the fridge for 30 minutes, or until required.

Preheat the oven to 180°C/350°F/gas mark 4. Grease a round 20cm/8 inch tart tin (pan) with a little butter.

Roll out the pastry on a lightly floured surface and use to line the greased tart tin. Cut off the trimmings and form them into a ball, then roll out and cut into 12 strips.

Fill the pastry case with the jam, then arrange the strips over the tart in a lattice pattern. Brush the strips with the beaten egg, then bake the tart for 25 minutes, until lightly golden.

Leave to cool slightly, then sprinkle with icing sugar and serve.

MAKES 25–30 BISCUITS

250g/9oz fine polenta (cornmeal)

100g/3$\frac{1}{2}$oz/$\frac{2}{3}$ cup cornflour
(cornstarch)

175g/6oz/generous $\frac{3}{4}$ cup caster
(superfine) sugar

finely grated zest of 1 orange

finely grated zest of 1 unwaxed lemon

175g/6oz/generous $\frac{3}{4}$ cup butter,
melted

2 eggs, beaten

Biscotti di polenta agli agrumi
Citrus polenta biscuits

Using polenta (cornmeal) in desserts has become fashionable, and it is often made into cakes and biscuits. Apart from being delicious, with that extra crunch that polenta flour gives, these biscuits are a perfect sweet treat for anyone suffering from wheat intolerance. Simple to make and quick to bake, they are an ideal accompaniment to ice cream (see Il gelato della nonna Fausta, page 204) or to enjoy with a cup of tea. Space them well apart on the baking tray, as they spread during cooking; if necessary, bake in batches.

Preheat the oven to 180°C/350°F/gas mark 4. Combine the polenta, cornflour, sugar and orange and lemon zests in a bowl. Make a well in the centre, pour in the melted butter and beaten eggs and stir well. Cover and refrigerate for 20 minutes, until it becomes a little firmer.

Line 2 large baking trays with non-stick greaseproof paper. Place $\frac{1}{2}$ tbsp dollops on the paper, spacing them at least 6cm/2$\frac{1}{2}$ inch apart. Bake for 12 minutes, until the edges turn golden. Leave to cool slightly before serving.

Torta di mela di Nonna Genoveffa

Granny Genoveffa's apple cake

SERVES 4–6

85g/3oz/6 tbsp unsalted softened butter, plus extra to grease

3 Granny Smith apples

juice and finely grated zest of 1 small unwaxed lemon

3 eggs

150g/5¹/₂oz/³/₄ cup caster (superfine) sugar

1 vanilla pod

300g/10¹/₂oz/generous 2 cups self-raising (self-rising) flour

---

This is a homely cake that, while baking, fills the house with a wonderful aroma. In the fall I would bring home basketfuls of apples and always made sure I gave lots to my grandma because I knew she would make this cake. She would bake several to give to family and friends. I gave the recipe to my wife Liz, who now makes it, and I can't tell you how quickly the slices disappear, often still warm. I have used Granny Smith apples, but any will suffice and if you prefer you can substitute pears, plums or apricots – a cake for every season.

Preheat the oven to 180°C/350°F/gas mark 4. Grease a round, 20cm/8 inch diameter, loose-bottomed cake tin (pan) with a little butter, then line with non-stick greaseproof paper.

Peel and core the apples, chop them into medium chunks and put them in a bowl. Squeeze over the lemon juice to avoid discolouration and set aside.

Whisk together the eggs and sugar in a large bowl until light and fluffy. Add the butter and whisk until well amalgamated. Split the vanilla pod with a sharp knife and scoop out the seeds with the tip of the knife, then add them to the bowl. Sift in the flour, then fold it in. Add and fold in the apples and lemon zest.

Pour the mixture into the prepared tin and bake for about 40 minutes, or until golden and springy to the touch. Remove from the oven and allow to cool in the tin. To serve, unmould from the tin and place on a serving plate. Slice and enjoy with tea or coffee.

Cassatine

Mini cassata cakes

MAKES 12 SMALL CASSATE

icing (confectioner's) sugar, sifted, to dust

350g/12oz marzipan

40ml/1½fl oz/scant 3 tbsp Marsala

sugared flowers, silver balls, angelica and
candied peel, to decorate

for the sponge
2 eggs

100g/3½oz/⅓ cup caster (superfine) sugar

75g/2¾oz/scant ½ cup plain
(all-purpose) flour, sifted

1 tsp baking powder, sifted

for the filling
100ml/3½fl oz/⅓ cup double (heavy) cream

200g/7oz ricotta

60g/2¼oz/generous ¼ cup caster
(superfine) sugar

85g/3oz candied peel

40g/1½oz plain (semisweet) chocolate drops
or finely chopped chocolate

This recipe is a labour of love. These cakes take time and patience to prepare, but believe me they're worth it. They are traditionally Sicilian, and were first introduced to our family by my Zia Maria. Her husband would often go on business to Sicily and return with tales of this wonderful dessert, and he once bought her kilos of Sicilian almonds. With what she was told and the almonds she had, she decided to give these a go – and what better occasion than my sister Filomena's wedding? Instead of making a large cake, she made hundreds of little ones, and beautifully decorated them all with flowers made of candied fruit; it took her at least 2 days. They were a joy to look at and tasted delicious. When you have made them, leave them overnight in the fridge – they are even more delectable when left to settle for a while.

For the sponge, follow the method for the Celebration cake on page 145, using a rectangular, 28 x 22cm/11 x 8½-inch non-stick cake tin (pan). Bake for 15 minutes, until golden and springy to the touch. Remove from the oven and leave to cool in the tin.

For the filling, whisk the cream until thick. In another bowl, whisk the ricotta and sugar together until creamy. Stir in the candied peel, chocolate and thickened cream. Cover and refrigerate for at least 30 minutes.

Line 12 x 6cm/2½-inch ovenproof bowls with clingfilm (plastic wrap). Dust a work surface with plenty of sifted icing sugar and roll out the marzipan to a thickness of 3mm/⅛ inch. Using a 10cm/4-inch cutter, cut out 12 rounds. Line the clingfilmed bowls with the marzipan rounds. Cut 12 pieces of the cooled sponge in the same way and place on top of the marzipan. Brush the sponge with Marsala, then divide the filling betweeen the bowls.

Using a 4cm/1½-inch cutter, cut out 12 rounds from the remaining sponge and place on top of the filling, pressing gently. Brush with the remaining Marsala. Reroll the marzipan if necessary, cut out rounds and place on top, then fold the clingfilm over to seal. Refrigerate for at least 2 hours, or until set.

Remove each *cassata* from the fridge, loosen the clingfilm and tip upside-down to unmould. Remove the clingfilm, transfer to a serving dish and decorate with sugared flowers, silver balls, angelica or candied peel.

Torta di Paolo

Paolo's cake

- - - - - - - - - - - - - - - - - - - -

SERVES 6

200g/7oz/scant 1 cup unsalted butter,
melted, plus extra to grease
4 eggs, separated
200g/7oz/1 cup caster (superfine) sugar
1 vanilla pod
150g/5½oz/1 cup plain (all-purpose) flour
50g/1¾oz/⅓ cup cornflour (cornstarch)
1 tsp baking powder
a pinch of salt
finely grated zest of 1 unwaxed lemon
icing (confectioners') sugar, sifted, to dust

- - - - - - - - - - - - - - - - - - - -

My good friend Paolo is an expert at making this traditional Italian cake, commonly known as *Torta Margherita* or *Paradiso*. This is his mother's recipe, which he has been recreating ever since he left home. Each time he makes this cake and brings it round, it disappears in no time. Simple to make, it is ideal with a cup of tea or even with a glass of Vin Santo after dinner.

Preheat the oven to 180°C/350°F/gas mark 4. Grease a round, 22cm/8½ inch diameter loose-bottomed cake tin with butter, then line with non-stick greaseproof paper.

Whisk together the egg yolks and sugar in a large bowl until almost white. Split the vanilla pod with a sharp knife and scoop out the seeds with the tip of the knife, then add them to the bowl. Sift in the flour, cornflour, baking powder and salt and gradually fold them in. Mix in the melted butter and lemon zest.

Whisk the egg whites in a clean, glass bowl until stiff peaks form, then gently fold into the egg yolk mixture.

Pour the mixture into the prepared tin and bake for 30–35 minutes, or until golden and springy to the touch. To check if the cake is cooked, insert a wooden skewer in the centre – if it comes out clean the cake is ready; if not cook for a few minutes longer. Allow to cool in the tin. Unmould on to a plate and sprinkle with sifted icing sugar.

Preserves

Preserving food has always been important in my kitchen. It is a way of keeping the scents and flavours of produce long after it is in season. When I was a child, our store cupboard was always full of jars of preserved bell peppers, aubergines (eggplant), courgettes (zucchini), mushrooms, green beans, artichokes, giardiniera (mixed vegetables), tomatoes, cherries, peaches and various fruit jams. We made most preserves ourselves, but friends and neighbours would come round with gifts of their own preserved goodies too.

The end of summer was a busy time for us, as the family prepared for the preservation of the beloved tomatoes. Kilos and kilos of them had to be bottled in order to give us a year-long supply. As well as bottling them, we sun-dried them and made concentrato (a very thick tomato paste). On balconies and terraces throughout our village, trays of salted tomatoes that had been sliced in half were dried in the hot sun. For the concentrato, they were put through a mincer to extract the pulp, which was then put in large, flat, terracotta dishes, covered with nets to keep the flies off, and placed in the sun. The mixture had to be stirred every couple of hours with a large wooden spoon and sprinkled with a little olive oil to prevent a crust from forming. The dishes were taken in at night and brought out again in the early morning for about 3 days, until the pulp had turned into a thick, delicious concentrate of pure tomato. It was then transferred into jars, drizzled with a little olive oil and stored. Just a little of this pure nectar was needed to make the most amazing ragù sauce for Sunday lunch. Not even the best shop-bought variety will ever match the flavour.

We preserved throughout the year, but mainly during spring, summer and fall. Aubergines, peppers, green beans and artichokes were placed in oil so that we could enjoy them later as antipasto or as a snack with bread. Peaches and cherries were preserved in syrup or alcohol or made into jam; figs were sun-dried and eaten at Christmas, and strawberries and end-of-summer berries were made into delicious jam to be eaten on bread or in my mother's crostate (tarts). We preserved all sorts of vegetables in pure wine vinegar to make our own version of giadiniera (see page 224). The vinegar was always our own, made with leftover wine that was poured into a large glass container to which a couple of pieces of dried pasta would be added – this helped to speed up the process of turning the wine into vinegar. We would leave the container open for about 20 days, gently shaking it daily, until the wine turned into the most pungent vinegar. The vinegar was then transferred into smaller bottles and sealed with a cork. I still do this at home today.

My mother even preserved her own tuna. When the fishermen caught this fish, word would spread around the village very quickly and housewives would assemble on the beach to buy pieces just for preserving. It involved a lengthy process of gently cooking the fish in salty water and then drying it, before placing it in jars with olive oil. The results were worthwhile and my mother made lots to keep in our store cupboard for quick, healthy meals. Families also preserved their own anchovies and sardines. A few years ago, when I was on holiday on the Sicilian island of Lipari, I preserved some anchovies and brought them home to enjoy at Christmas – the taste was amazing and reminded us of being back on the sunny island.

Preserving food doesn't just lock away its freshness; as you enjoy it, memories of where you were when you ate it, what time of year it was, who you were with and, maybe, even what you were talking or thinking about while you were doing the preserving will flood back.

We now find all sorts of produce all year round, but I still like to preserve. During autumn when we go mushroom-picking, and I love to preserve porcini (ceps) or chiodini (honeyfungus), which we enjoy having with our Christmas lunch antipasto, as well as giving away as presents. Liz's favourite is preserved aubergines and peppers, which again we enjoy as antipasto. My friend Paolo also loves to preserve, and at the end of summer, when his allotment flourishes, he comes bearing gifts of delicious fruit jams and mixed pickle. I hope this tradition does not die away; I certainly keep it alive and hope my young daughters will do the same when they are older.

Preserving basics

- Always use very fresh, good-quality fruit and vegetables that are in season.

- To sterilize jars: wash and thoroughly clean all the jars you are going to use, then rinse out with a little white wine vinegar. Leave to drain, then dry well. If you are using new jars, after washing them place in a large pan of boiling water and boil for a couple of minutes. Remove, drain and dry well.

- To pasteurize: once you have placed the preserves in jars, seal well, preferably using hermetically sealed lids. Wrap each jar in old kitchen cloths – this prevents it from breaking during boiling. Line a large pan with kitchen cloth. Place the wrapped jars in it and add enough cold water to cover them by 3cm/1 inch. Bring the water to the boil, then reduce the heat to medium and boil for the time stated in the recipe. Turn off the heat, but leave the jars in the water until it is cold. Remove the jars and unwrap, then dry with a clean cloth, label and place in the store cupboard.

12 long, thin, sweet green (bell) peppers, about 350g/12oz in total

400ml/14fl oz/1³/₄ cups white wine vinegar or preserving vinegar

20 black peppercorns

6 bay leaves

1 litre/1³/₄ pint/4 cups olive oil or good sunflower oil

for the filling

150–160g/5¹/₂ oz canned tuna in oil, drained (keeping a little oil aside)

20g/³/₄oz capers, finely chopped

9 anchovy fillets in oil, drained and finely chopped

Peperoni dolci ripieni sott'olio

Preserved filled sweet peppers

I love these long, thin, sweet green peppers, known as *friggitelli* in Campania. I usually buy them in Greek or Turkish shops and find they are slightly larger than the Italian ones; however, the sweet, delicate taste is similar and they are ideal for stuffing. When I find them, I buy lots, fill them with tuna and preserve them in oil so I can enjoy them as picked, as a little antipasto or light meal with bread. In Italy, my mother would fill and preserve tiny bell peppers at the end of summer.

Sterilize jars with a total volume of 2 litres/3¹/₂ pints/ 8 cups (see page 221) and dry thoroughly with a clean tea towel.

Using a small sharp knife, make a slit lengthways down one side of each pepper, then carefully remove the seeds and any white bits.

Place the vinegar in a pan and bring to the boil, then add a few peppers at a time and boil for 2 minutes, turning them over halfway through. Drain and leave to dry on kitchen towel.

Meanwhile, combine all the ingredients for the filling, adding a little of the tuna oil if necessary for binding.

Fill the peppers and place in the sterilized jars. Drop in the peppercorns and bay leaves and pour in the oil, making sure the peppers are covered. Secure with a vinegar-proof lid, and pasteurize for 30 minutes (see page 221). Label and store in a cool, dark, dry place for about 1 month before using. Once opened, store in the fridge.

Giardiniera

Mixed vegetable pickle

- -

MAKES ABOUT 2 X 450ML/16FL OZ/ 1³/₄-CUP JARS

250ml/9fl oz/generous 1 cup white
wine vinegar

12 black peppercorns

2 cloves

4 bay leaves

1¹/₂ tsp salt

2 carrots, cut into chunks

1 celery heart, cut into chunks

140g/5oz cauliflower florets

125g/4¹/₂oz green beans, topped and
tailed and halved

1 small red (bell) pepper, deseeded and
cut into thin strips lengthways

1 small yellow (bell) pepper, deseeded
and cut into thin strips lengthways

140g/5oz baby (pearl) onions, peeled

140g/5oz aubergine (eggplant),
peeled and cut into strips

85g/3oz green olives, pitted and halved

¹/₂ tsp dried oregano

4 red chillies (chiles), left whole

350ml/12fl oz/1¹/₂ cups olive oil, plus extra
to top up if necessary

- -

Giardiniera is a classic Italian mixed vegetable pickle. It was traditionally made by farmers using the season's new vegetables. In many families it was traditional to fill a large *tinozza* (wooden container) with wine vinegar, and each day put in whatever vegetable you could find. The vinegar preserved them and we enjoyed them as pickled vegetables throughout the winter. At home, my mother would religiously make jars of *giardiniera* at the end of summer, which we would use to enhance the famous *rinforzo* (cauliflower) salad at Christmas.

Sterilize 2 x 450ml/16fl oz/1³/₄-cup jars (see page 221) and dry thoroughly with a clean tea towel.

Put 250ml/9fl oz/generous 1 cup water into a large pan and add the vinegar, peppercorns, cloves, bay leaves and salt. Bring to the boil. Add the carrots, celery and cauliflower, lower the heat slightly and simmer for 10 minutes. Remove with a slotted spoon and place on a clean tea towel to cool.

Add the green beans to the vinegar solution and cook for 4 minutes, then remove and leave to cool on the tea towel.

Add the peppers and onions and cook for 3 minutes, then transfer to the tea towel. Finally, add the aubergine and cook for 1 minute. Remove and leave all the vegetables to dry out and cool.

Put all the vegetables in a large bowl, add the olives, oregano, chillies and olive oil and mix. Leave to infuse for a couple of minutes, then carefully, without breaking the vegetables, fill the sterilized jars, pressing gently down with your fingers so the olive oil covers all the vegetables. Leave to rest for a minute and, if necessary, add some more oil. Seal with vinegar-proof lids and pasteurize for 30 minutes (see page 221). Leave to cool, then label and store in a cool, dry, dark cupboard for about 1 week before using. Once opened, store in the fridge.

MAKES 2 X 400ML/14FL OZ/ 1¾-CUP JAR

2 large aubergines (eggplant), about 900g/2lb total weight

salt

700ml/1¼ pints/2¾ cups white wine vinegar or preserving vinegar

300ml/10fl oz/1¼ cups olive oil or good sunflower oil, plus a little extra if necessary to top up

2 garlic cloves, thinly sliced

½ large red chilli (chile), thinly sliced

2 tsp dried oregano

Melanzane sott'olio
Preserved aubergines

My family loves this tasty way of preserving aubergines (eggplant). My wife Liz always makes a large quantity to be enjoyed at Christmas with our antipasto of cured meats. Everyone who tries them wants the recipe. My pregnant daughter-in-law, Judith, phoned one evening for the recipe in desperation to satisfy her craving! They really are tasty and make a delicious midnight snack on good country bread.

Sterilize 2 x 400ml/14fl oz/1¾-cup jars (see page 221) and dry thoroughly with a clean tea towel.

Peel the aubergines and cut lengthways into thin strips. Line a plastic container with the aubergine strips, sprinkle with a good handful of salt, then continue layering the aubergine and salt. Cover with greaseproof paper, place a weight on top and leave for 1 hour. During this time, the aubergines will exude quite a bit of water. Squeeze out the excess liquid, return to the containers and cover with the vinegar, then with the clingfilm. Leave for a further 1 hour.

Drain the aubergines, squeezing out the excess vinegar with your hands. Place in a bowl with the oil, garlic, chilli and oregano and mix well, then fill the sterilized jars. Pack the aubergines snugly and, if necessary, top up with a little more oil. Secure with a vinegar-proof lid and, if you wish to keep them for some time, pasteurize for 20 minutes (see page 221). Otherwise, label and place in a cool, dry place for about 3 days before consuming. Once opened, store in the fridge.

Pomodori conservati a casa

Preserved tomatoes

**MAKES ABOUT 4 X 500ML/18FL OZ/
GENEROUS 2-CUP JARS**

1.5kg/3lb 5oz tomatoes, preferably San
Marzano or small plum tomatoes
a large handful of fresh basil leaves

Preserving tomatoes was an annual family ritual
when I was a child – in fact, most people in our
village would do it at the end of summer, when the
local San Marzano tomato was plentiful. Lengthy
preparations were made for it. I helped with
gathering empty beer bottles and corks; a large
table was set up in the garden with chairs around
it for the production line to begin, and a big old oil
drum was placed over a fire for the pasteurization
process. We would preserve enough tomatoes to
give us a year-long supply. Sometimes, when I'm
lucky enough to get a glut of plum tomatoes at the
end of summer, I like to carry on the tradition – of
course, not in such a big way, but if I can get a
dozen or so jars in my store cupboard, I'm happy.

Sterilize 4 x 500ml/18fl oz/generous 2-cup jars (see
page 221) and dry thoroughly with a clean tea towel.

Halve or quarter the tomatoes (depending on their
size) and use them to fill the jars, adding the odd
basil leaf here and there. As you do this, gently press
the tomatoes down and pack them in. Seal with
the lids and pasteurize for 30 minutes (see page
221)., then remove them from the pan, leave to cool,
then label and store in a dark, dry cupboard. Once
opened, store in the fridge.

MAKES 4 X 400ML/14FL OZ/1^{3}/4 CUP JARS

1kg/2lb 4oz peaches, peeled, pitted
and cut into eighths

juice of 1 lemon

100g/3^{1}/₂oz/^{1}/₂ cup caster
(superfine) sugar

- - - - - - - - - - - - - - - -

Pesche sciroppate

Peaches in syrup

During summer, when peaches were plentiful, our family friend, Maria Gatto, who lived in the hills above Minori, would always preserve them. Her vast garden was full of fruit trees, vegetables and herbs – produce she would use in her cooking. She was always cooking for her elderly husband and 6 children. She would spend entire days in her kitchen and work late into the night to create wonderful recipes and make pots and pots of delicious preserves. Whenever my mother went to see her, she would return home laden with jars of Maria's specialities. We would enjoy her peaches later in the year, when they were no longer in season, and use them in cakes or simply enjoy them in their lovely syrup.

Sterilize 4 x 400ml/14fl oz/1^{3}/₄-cup jars (see page 221) and dry thoroughly with a clean tea towel.

Put the peaches into a bowl with the lemon juice and set aside.

Heat 500ml/18fl oz/generous 2 cups water in a saucepan with the sugar. Remove from the heat and leave to cool.

Drain the peaches and use them to fill the sterilized jars. Pour the cooled syrup over them, making sure you cover them completely. Secure with the lids.

Pasteurize for 1 minute (see page 221), then remove from the pan and leave to cool. Label and store in a cool, dry, dark cupboard until required. Once opened, store in the fridge.

**MAKES 2 X 250ML/9FL OZ/
GENEROUS 1-CUP JARS**

800g/1lb 12oz strawberries, hulled and
quartered

440g/15½oz/generous 2 cups caster
(superfine) sugar

juice of 1 lemon

Marmellata di fragole

Strawberry jam

This is my mum's strawberry jam, which she made each year in May when strawberries were plentiful. I would collect the small wild strawberries, *fragoline*, that covered the hills above Minori. I had to resist eating too many of them on the way home because if I didn't bring enough my mum wouldn't make her delicious jam. I loved to watch her make it and was sometimes allowed to stir it, but the best treat of all was that she always let me have some of it warm on bread to test. Once potted, the jam was stored in the cupboard and she would use it to fill her delicious *crostata* (see page 210). This is a really simple recipe, made in no time, and so much better and more nutritious than any shop-bought variety.

Sterilize 2 x 250ml/9fl oz/generous 1-cup jars (see page 221) and dry thoroughly with a clean tea towel. Put a saucer in the freezer, for testing the jam later.

Place all the ingredients in a saucepan, bring to the boil and simmer on a medium heat for 20–30 minutes, stirring from time to time. To test if the jam is ready, place a little on a cold saucer – if it sets, it is ready.

Remove from the heat, fill the sterilized jars and seal with the lids. Pasteurize for 30 minutes (see page 221), Immediately place upside-down until cool. label and store in a cool, dry place and use when required. Once opened, store in the fridge.

1.5kg/3lb 5oz damsons

300g/10$\frac{1}{2}$oz/1$\frac{1}{2}$ cups caster
(superfine) or granulated sugar

5 cloves

2 bay leaves

700ml/1$\frac{1}{4}$ pints/2$\frac{3}{4}$ cups pure grain
alcohol (available from good
Italian delis)

Susine selvatiche sotto spirito

Damsons in alcohol

I was in the country with my friend Paolo, cutting branches for my walking sticks, when we spotted a tree full of damsons. Of course, we had to pick them and, once home, I decided to preserve them in alcohol like we used to do in Italy. With his share, Paolo made jam, which we now enjoy with toast for our breakfast.

Sterilize 5 x 500ml/18fl oz/generous 2-cup jars (see page 221) and dry thoroughly with a clean tea towel.

Prick the damsons all over with a pin and set aside. Place 350ml/12fl oz/1$\frac{1}{2}$ cups water in a saucepan with the sugar, cloves and bay leaves. Cook over a medium heat until the sugar has dissolved. Remove from the heat and stir in the alcohol.

Fill the sterilized jars with the damsons, pour the liquid over them, making sure you cover them completely, and leave for a couple of minutes until the bubbles subside. Secure with the lids, label and leave for 3 months in a cool, dry, dark place before using. Once opened, store in the fridge.

**MAKES 2 X 500ML/18FL OZ/
GENEROUS 2-CUP JARS**

500g/1lb 2oz good cherries

225g/8oz/generous 1 cup caster
(superfine) or granulated sugar

300ml/10fl oz/1¼ cups pure grain
alcohol (available from good
Italian delis)

Ciliegie sotto spirito

Cherries preserved in alcohol

Cherries are the first hint that summer really is on its way! I always look forward to seeing the trees in full bloom and the market stalls being piled high with the succulent fruit. Every year my father preserved cherries in alcohol so we could enjoy them later in the winter months. I do the same and look forward to opening a jar around Christmas time and enjoying a little taste of summer with a slice of cake.

Sterilize 2 x 500ml/18fl oz/2-cup jars (see page 221) and dry thoroughly with a clean tea towel. Put a saucer in the freezer, for testing the jam later.

Trim the cherry stems, leaving on about a quarter of their length. Prick the cherries all over with a pin.

Place 300ml/10fl oz/1¼ cups water in a saucepan with the sugar. Put over a medium heat and stir until the sugar has dissolved. Remove from the heat and stir in the alcohol.

Fill the sterilized jars with the cherries and pour in the liquid, making sure you cover them completelly. Leave to cool, then secure with the lids and label. Leave for about 3 months in a cool, dry, dark place before using. Once opened, store in the fridge.

Index

Acknowledgements

Liz Przybylski for ghostwriting the book and organising me. Adriana for testing the recipes and cooking at the photo shoots. David Loftus for the outstanding photographs. Sara Mulvanny for the gorgeous illustrations. Georgina Hewitt for the art direction and design and Miranda Harvey for laying it all out. Paolo Baietti for helping at the photo shoots. Barbara for editing and correcting. Becca Spry at Pavilion for overseeing the project. Chloe, Olivia, Eoin Dylan and Freddie for being fabulous at the shoot. Luigi Bonomi, my agent.